THE SATIRES OF PERSIUS

THE SATIRES OF PERSIUS

translated by W. S. MERWIN

introduction & notes by William S. Anderson

KENNIKAT PRESS
Port Washington, N. Y./London

THE SATIRES OF PERSIUS

Published in 1973 by Kennikat Press by
arrangement with Indiana University Press
Library of Congress Catalog Card No.: 72-85278
ISBN 0-8046-1708-2

Manufactured by Taylor Publishing Company Dallas, Texas

CONTENTS

LINE REFERENCES IN THE INTRODUCTION AND IN THE RUNNING HEADS ARE TO THE LATIN TEXT IN THE LOEB EDITION.

INTRODUCTION

THE POET who dies young after a brief life of dedication to his craft has always been a congenial figure to our imaginations, for we naturally tend to conjecture what might have become of him had he survived to the age of a Sophocles or his modern counterpart, Robert Frost. Aules Persius Flaccus died at 28, long before he had completed his work, leaving a small body of poems which constitute some of the most revolutionary writing in an age of ceaseless literary experiment. What might have happened to Roman poetry, especially Roman satire, had he reached the age of forty or fifty or more, we can never know. Juvenal, the man who gave the ultimate direction to Roman satire, learned much from Persius' work and as a middle-aged man produced satires whose mature art has never been successfully challenged.

There are few Roman poets of whom we possess an authoritative biography; Persius is one of those few. Within thirty years of his death, the scholar Valerius Probus had collected a small body of independent data and appended these details to an edition of Persius' works. Persius was born in the city then known as Volaterra, located on the western coast of Italy about midway between Rome and modern Genoa; the year was A.D. 34, late in the reign of Tiberius, a few years after the crucifixion of Jesus of Nazareth. Volaterra belonged among the early settlements of the Etruscans, and, although the Etruscans had ceased to exert any power or influence in Italy for centuries, those who could trace their Etruscan ancestry, real or imagined, were quick to point the fact out to others less privileged. To judge from the name Aules, Persius may well have belonged among these Etruscans. If so, he knew the emptiness of title: in III, *27* ff. he ridicules the pretensions of "a descendant (number one thousand) of some Tuscan ancestor." It may be that Volaterra fostered a spirit of political independence in its children. Persius himself never involved himself in the court scandals of his time, and Paetus Thrasea, his compatriot and relative, a Volaterranian who symbolized the best moral ideals of the Neronian Age, courted death rather than the servile life of most Roman senators.

By birth, Persius belonged to the upper classes, unlike the more famous poets of the Augustan Age, Horace and Virgil. His family possessed the property qualifications to make him a knight; besides, he was linked by relationship and marriage to the Senatorial class. Persius' father died when the boy was six; his mother re-married, but this husband soon died also. Although in III, *47* the satirist talks of a father attending his recitation, and not with much respect, this incident seems to be imaginary. The principal influence in Persius' early years accordingly must have been his mother and her family. Thus, it was an important event of Persius' youth when in 42 Caecina Paetus was ordered to commit suicide and Arria, his wife and possibly Persius' aunt, certainly a close relative, gave Caecina a lesson in bravery by stabbing herself and saying: "See Paetus, it does not hurt!" This took place early in the reign of Claudius, ruler throughout Persius' adolescence, a man whom an ascetic like Persius could never respect, especially since as a student in Rome Persius had ample opportunity to observe the emperor's absurdities.

At the age of 12, that is, in 46, Persius went to Rome, to study with the best teachers of the day: the eminent grammarian Remmius Palaemon, who must have communicated to his pupil some of his fanatic love of language; Verginius Flavus, the rhetorician; and finally, the most influential of all his instructors, Annaeus Cornutus. Persius first acquired Cornutus' friendship at the age of sixteen, a dangerous age for most young men, and to judge from the description in v, 30 ff., Persius was no exception. It is generally believed that Cornutus belonged to the household of Seneca, probably as a freedman. We cannot tell whether Cornutus brought Persius into contact with Seneca's family, or whether Persius' circle of friends already included the Annaei and through them he found the man whom he would ever after regard as his master and friend. At any rate, by providing us the date of the friendship (A.D. 49-50), the biography serves to remind us of the new position of Seneca and family in court.

As Tacitus interpreted Claudius' reign, it fell into two parts: from near the beginning to 48, Claudius doddered along, falling more and more under the influence of the sexually perverse Messalina; after Messalina's execution he all too quickly married his niece Agrippina, whose lust centered on power and who eventually disposed of Claudius in 54, to make room for her son and what she fondly expected to be her own dominance of Rome. One of the first acts performed by Claudius after marrying Agrippina in 49 consisted of the recall of Seneca from exile in Corsica, where he had languished for six years after incurring the emperor's wrath. Agrippina had plans for Seneca: he was to change the popular image of the reign, and he was to act as tutor for her son (the later Nero) by an earlier marriage. Thus, Persius meets Cornutus precisely at the point when the star of Seneca, Cornutus' former owner, is rising; and, had his interests been different, he might well have been drawn into the exciting political intrigues with Seneca and his family. Another young man of sixteen in A.D. 50 might well have felt attracted by the masterful scheme of Agrippina, a woman of beauty and intelligence, if devoid of scruples; another young man might have joined the festivities four years later when the news of the "death" of Claudius was announced. Persius shunned politics; his writings are permeated with a loathing for the shallow interests of the court circles. He came to know both Seneca and his brilliant nephew Lucan, but neither won his admiration or friendship.

We tend to think of Seneca as the representative Stoic of his age; his so-called Stoic tragedies exercised an incalculably important influence upon Elizabethan drama. Seneca's Stoicism, like his whole career, consisted of compromises; he was, in fact, a thorough eclectic, and for that very reason one of the most sympathetic of all Stoics to the average reader, but for the same reason one of the least typical Stoics. When he rejected Seneca's political intrigues, Persius also repudiated Seneca's eclectic brand of Stoicism and turned to a much more strict doctrine, as inculcated by Cornutus and lived by such uncompromising friends as Paetus Thrasea. It may perhaps be a mark of his youth, but his surviving writings pulsate with religious enthusiasm for the most extreme and paradoxical tenets of the Porch. By the time of his death, he had amassed some seven hundred volumes of the works of Chrysippus, the most prolific Stoic writer; other treatises he obviously had studied minutely with Cornutus. Committed as he was to Stoicism, Persius set out to communicate his enthusiasm, like an evangelical preacher exposing the errors of mankind and pointing to the one and only Way by which to escape personal disaster. Not an expert philosopher but excited by the metaphysical possibilities of his sect, Persius limited his interest to practical moral lessons, the basic tenets upon which a secure existence may be founded. While we must think of him as a Stoic satirist, we should be careful to distinguish between the philosopher-like Cornutus and the inspired pupil Persius who sets out to popularize a few of the more prominent and immediately apprehensible beliefs of the school. There is nothing original or even striking in the Stoicism that confronts us in the Satires; but Stoic satire like that of Persius is new.

Cornutus enjoyed a reputation in that period as a tragedian rather than as a philosopher. Consequently, the circle of friends which collected around this seemingly irresistible personality consisted about equally of poets and philosophers, or those who combined an interest in Stoicism with poetic talent by producing much of the Stoic poetry that marks the literature of this period. Among the older men, in addition to Cornutus himself and Seneca, we should mention Caesius Bassus, a lyric poet whom a critic like Quintilian would rank second only to Horace; Bassus would one day serve as the literary executor of Persius' Satires. Younger than Persius, but also a pupil of Cornutus, was Seneca's nephew Lucan, one of the most talented poets of all time, like Persius cut off by premature death. Literary discussions, recitations of works, mutual constructive criticism, must have formed as important an element of this circle's existence as its deep concern with Stoicism. We know that Cornutus wrote treatises on orthography and on the allegorization of myth; that Bassus also speculated on orthographical principles; that Paetus Thrasea composed an important biography of Cato; and the wide interests of Seneca emerge in the variety of his many writings. Thus, when we read Satire 1, we can easily imagine ourselves participating in the literary controversies of the time, a member of a close circle of Stoic poets who find the style and material of the court poets utterly offensive. It is almost a manifesto denouncing the taste of Neronian society.

It is most unlikely that Persius composed any of these Satires during the reign of Claudius, who, while he stimulated interest in scholarship and himself could be ranked as a capable historian and Etruscologist, did not promote literature in general, least of all poetry. With the accession of Nero, a change seemed in prospect, for Nero had been trained by Seneca to regard himself as the hope of culture, the introducer of a new Golden Age to rival that of Augustus. The contrast Seneca develops in his *Apocolocyntosis* between the stuttering pedantry of Claudius and the Apolline inspiration of the new ruler seems to have been part of the propaganda of the time. Indeed, in some respects, the young Nero did react brilliantly against the ways of his step-father, above all in his encouragement of, and participation in, literary endeavors. Around him he gathered a group of young artists, poets, dramatists, and musicians, Roman and Greek, and for a while the court became the center of literary activity. What was missing in all this—and what accordingly gave Neronian literature an inferior place in the total mass of Latin writing—was a moral basis, a dedication to the well-being of Rome, a positive mission in politics as well as in poetry. One could write about the New Age only so long, before the enormities of Nero's licentiousness created the inevitable conflict in one's mind, and one ended either as a servile court poet, like Calpurnius Piso, or as an implacable foe of the ruler, like Lucan and his Stoic companions. A vein of criticism, dissatisfaction, runs through the best literature of the Neronian Age: witness the *Satyricon* of Petronius, the tragedies of Seneca, the *Pharsalia* of Lucan, and the Satires of Persius. A poet could not, as in Augustus' day, regret certain features of the new regime, but in general be inspired by the magnificence of the total purpose; nothing in Nero's purpose gave confidence to the men who watched him dallying with poetry, especially when he could so openly humiliate Lucan, a better poet than himself.

Persius must have begun writing his satires near the end of Nero's first five years, around 58 or 59, by which time the spell of youthful brilliance had worn thin and the true perversity of Nero showed through. It is unnecessary to recite the series of ruthless crimes and reckless acts which Nero, now breaking free from his tutors and advisors, committed in these next years; one has only to read Tacitus' account of the murder of Agrippina, then of Octavia, to feel the chill of disappointment. Others began to publish anonymous lampoons against this parricide; Persius divorced himself utterly from specific events and tried to comment on the timeless, but ever timely, human failures such as avarice and luxury, faults that lay heavily upon the nobility and freedmen of his day. He must have been in ill health even then, for much that he writes sounds as though it came second hand, filtered through from his conversations and readings but rendered in that inimitable style of his. Where Seneca describes precisely public activities like the gladiatoral shows, the baths, recitations, and the like; where Petronius abounds in minute details, based on intimate observation, of Trimalchio's and other freedmen's ways, Persius contents himself with a general reference to a typical, not a specific, behavior. Living much in the society of his mother and sister, or that of Cornutus and other Stoic men of letters, he successfully insulated himself from the lurid activity of court and wrote slowly away.

Nero had not yet reached his nadir when Persius died of a stomach ailment in 62. A few years later, the Pisonian Conspiracy would permit the emperor to wipe out the Stoic Circle in which Persius found so much inspiration: Seneca, presumably guiltless, would be forced to commit suicide; his nephew and Persius' fellow pupil, Lucan, quite guilty, would meet the same fate melodramatically; Cornutus, Musonius Rufus, and Demetrius, three of the most influential Stoic or cynic teachers, would be sent into exile. The climax of Nero's murderous career would, in the words of Tacitus, be the attack on virtue herself, namely, the liquidation of Barea Soranus, then of Paetus Thrasea. It is certainly quite possible that, had Persius lived three years longer, he might have shared the fate of his friends; for a tradition persists that remarks against the emperor had crept into his Satires, as they had into the *Pharsalia* of Lucan. So much we can state or reasonably assume about Persius' life in the times of Claudius and Nero.

Probus' biography provides us a list of Persius' works, a very brief one. As a young man Persius produced a tragedy which has disappeared. Another youthful work in one book also remains lost and titleless because of corruption in our Manuscripts. Then the death of Arria, wife of Caecina Paetus, who gave her husband the example of a brave suicide, as already mentioned, inspired a certain number of verses; these, too, have disappeared, all suppressed by the advice of Cornutus to Persius' mother. We do not definitely know Cornutus' reason, but it seems safe to assume that Persius' *juvenilia* did him no especial credit as a poet, and his affectionate old master wisely chose to entrust Persius' future reputation to his Satires.

Comparison of the titles of Persius' youthful poetry with those of his contemporary Lucan, on whom we are also well informed, proves instructive. Lucan wrote a great deal more and far more frivolously; he was at first among the poetic circle around Nero, and the titles of his works well illustrate the fact. From the beginning, Persius used his poems to express serious ideas; his tragedy was based on some episode from Roman history, and his verses on Arria must have pulsated with admiration for her moral bravery. Thus, whereas Lucan's gradual withdrawal from the mellifluous insipidity of court poetry to the thundering tones of his Stoic epic represents a definite change—one, in fact, which Probus attributes to the influence of Persius—Persius wrote consistently with a moral severity, though in different genres. It was not, however, until he experimented in satire that he discovered the form which would permit him the maximum poetic development.

Appended to Probus' authoritative biography, obviously later and of uncertain value, are a number of lines which purport to tell how Persius began his career as a satirist. When he left school, the lines say, Persius began to read Lucilius. It was Book X of Lucilius that shook him into action; Lucilius' sardonic comments on the poets of 120 B.C. impelled Persius to write a similar poem, bringing Lucilius up to date and attacking the vapid poetry and rhetoric of Neronian times. The unreliability of these details can be readily indicated: Persius finished "school" at the age of sixteen, a good four years before Nero became ruler and long before the character of his reign could be ascertained; furthermore, scholars do not unanimously agree that Satire 1, the poem in which Persius launches his attack on contemporary literature, is his earliest satire. However, for us there is one important detail which bears further investigation: namely, that Persius' inspiration came from Lucilius and specifically from Lucilius' Book X. Who this Lucilius was and what Roman satire was as it emerged from his hands and those of his capable successor Horace introduces the question: why did Persius find satire so congenial a form for his poetic efforts?

When we today speak of satire, we generally refer to a manner rather than a precise form; contemporary novels and movies are correctly called satires of certain customs or institutions. Almost anything can be satiric if it ridicules. There was a time in early Rome when *satura* (the Latin equivalent for our term) possessed great vagueness also, but of a quite different nature. Scholars have attempted to determine the origin of the Latin word, on the basis of random comments in later writers and our earliest specimens of *satura*, with no certain results. The majority favor the theory that *satura* comes from the adjective *satur* and originally meant "that which is full"; in other words, it denoted a certain style of writing in which several different forms were mixed, for example, drama and epic, several different meters, or meter and prose. Another more recent, hence less prevalent, theory depends upon the results of efforts to translate the Etruscan language. Less than fifteen years ago, the Etruscan word *satr-satir*—was deciphered by an Italian scholar as meaning "to say." Now if *satura* be regarded as originally an Etruscan word—and good arguments for this can be developed—then we find that the basic conception of the term is one of conversation; and it is certainly true that dialogue and informal discourse constitute its regular manner of poetic presentation. Whether we regard *satura* as basically a mixture or a conversation, the fact remains that the primary quality which we attribute to satire and which later Romans found in their *satura*, namely, the element of personal criticism, was not a definitive feature of pre-literary "satire." Instead, it possessed a loose dramatic, conversational, vaguely metrical form which was capable of, and would eventually receive, considerable development.

The first name to be clearly associated with *satura* is that of the great early Latin poet Ennius. While achieving fame as a tragedian, creating the form for the Latin epic, and experimenting in many poetic areas where Greek writers had led the way, Ennius wrote several books which, as a collection, were entitled *Saturae*. From the few fragments—some thirty lines in various meters—surviving, we can hardly describe his achievement. However, to judge from the comments of later critics, Ennius attained little note with his Satires; by comparison with the brilliant originality and fruitfulness of his other works, especially his *Annales*, the Satires were virtually negligible. Roman writers discussing *satura* either entirely ignore Ennius or relegate him to a minor place by comparison with Lucilius and Horace. Therefore, while Ennius' *satura* may have possessed in embryo some features of later *satura*, in the form of mixture, informality, social criticism, and the like, it lacked that strong personal assertiveness which Lucilius introduced, for which Lucilius is described by Horace as the "inventor" of satire.

Gaius Lucilius inherited a number of literary traditions, from comedy, epic, lyric, diatribe, and the like, and blended them into a new and highly versatile genre, whose most outstanding feature was the strong personal approach of the poet or his *persona*. Later generations thought of Lucilius, who produced his Satires at the end of the Second Century B.C., as the supreme exponent of invective; the "Lucilian character" became proverbial for the sharp personal attack. Accordingly, Persius in I, *114* ff., reviewing the approaches of his predecessors in this genre, automatically thinks of Lucilius first and describes him as follows:

> Lucilius took
> The skin off this city; he flayed you, Lupus, and you,
> Mucius, and ground you till his molars broke.

Rutilius Lupus and Mucius Scaevola were two of the most prominent Senators in Rome between 130 and 115 B.C. Now, to attack men of such standing, one must either be their equal or indulge in the type of political lampoon which, even if anonymous, involves one in many dangers. Lucilius belonged to a respectable and wealthy family which achieved senatorial status at least during his lifetime, if not before. His brother became a Senator; Lucilius himself counted Scipio Africanus Minor and Laelius as his closest friends; and his niece allied the family with the ambitious Pompey, father of Caesar's great rival. As the peer of those he attacked, the satirist could afford to exercise his freedom. And this freedom manifested itself in several ways: in the savagery of his invective, as we have said, in the diversity of his interests, in unashamed confessions, and in a relaxed but dignified style. The sum total of these qualities constitutes Lucilian *libertas*; it was the error of shallow critics to limit Lucilius' contributions and originality to invective.

To return to the passage interpolated in the biography of Persius, we observed that it credited to Book X of Lucilius Persius' inspiration to write Satire 1. A quick reading of the Satire will demonstrate that Persius takes no interest in political topics, and indeed Lucilius X made its topic not politics but the state of literature in contemporary Rome of 120 B.C. Although we possess but a few fragments of Lucilius' poem, we can pretty well assume that the satirist's freedom manifested itself in a sharp commentary on the poets and orators of his day, ending perhaps with an implicit or explicit contrast, as Persius does, in which he stated his own ideal. Politics and literature represent but a small portion of Lucilius' interests: we possess other fragments on history, philosophy, military engagements, comic anecdotes, the latest scandal, etc. Or Lucilius might start from some incident which purportedly belonged to his experiences. We have many poems developing his theories—not altogether consistent, as is the case with many men—on the control and use of one's sexual drive. In the course of these, he frankly gives us details about his various mistresses and the catamites he has known, pronounces a misanthropic verdict on marriage, ridicules a poor henpecked husband; all of which has led some credulous scholars to attribute to Lucilius what his *persona* states and so define the satirist as a misogynist or libertine, depending on the details selected as evidence. Perhaps this suffices to illustrate the diversity of topics and approaches in Lucilian satire. And this diversity of material was presented in a poetic style unique for its time, a relaxed, informal, supremely lucid style, colloquial but never vulgar, dignified but never grandiose, a witty manner which became known as the Plain Style.

When we combine all these separate features—versatile material, elastically rich style, and strong personal stamp—we have the essence of Lucilian satire: hexameter poetry of personal moral criticism. It must be remembered that poetry was the primary purpose of the satirist. The *satura* which Lucilius invented aroused admiration and imitation because it was essentially poetry—on permanent moral topics. The ethical criticism which a satirist pronounces rarely reaches beyond the level of insight attained by the moral preachers and philosophers; and so it is a misconception to approach satire as essentially a document of moral protest, or a mirror of society.

In the First Century B.C., when lyric and elegiac, as well as satiric, poetry became the rage, Lucilius was properly regarded as one of the foremost Latin writers. This was at a time when there were many great personal poets; but in the First Century the greatest, beyond question, was Quintus Horatius Flaccus. Horace came from a much lower social stratum than Lucilius, and consequently could not exploit Lucilian freedom. His brief venture into politics as a young man ended in the battle of Philippi, when he fought on the losing side. So he returned to Rome and tried to re-build his life, now that his property had disappeared and his political hopes vanished. Finding a minor but responsible post in the civil service, he spent all his spare time developing a poetic interest which heretofore had received scant attention. Slowly he won the esteem of the patrons and men of letters, and slowly his subjects changed from the outright abuse of the Epodes to the lyric self-control of the Odes. Midway in the scale of his poetic development came the two books of *Sermones* or Satires, which are the first complete satiric poetry which has survived.

If we pause to reflect on the relative position of *satura* among Horace's poetic production, we may see confirmed what has been stated: that the hexameter satire of Lucilius struck the observant Romans because of its poetic merits. To voice his personal abuse—or rather the bitter hatreds of the Civil War period—Horace used the iambic epode, not Satire. When he began to see deeper into the moral problems of a convulsed age, he moved into a higher form of poetry, one which permitted mature personal reflection and a tone of serious, but by no means passionate, engagement, with the many opportunities for variation which have always characterized that versatile genre *satura*. Horace's Satires were the preparation for his inimitable Odes.

We have already cited Persius' reference to Lucilius; the same passage continues with a picture of Horace, also useful for us:

> And sly Horace
> Could tease his way into the guts of his laughing friend
> And touch the fault there; he had a trick of sticking out
> His nose and hanging people on it.

Despite the curious way Persius chooses to render the image of his predecessor, it is evident that he conceives of Horace as a much gentler critic than Lucilius, one who drives directly to the moral heart without offending his friends. The Horatian manner is defined much more succinctly by Horace himself as "laughingly to tell the truth," but Persius' comment suffices to show how successful Horace was. If we think of Lucilius as the Roman aristocrat calmly stating his opinions, regardless of possible prejudice or bias, among a group of his equals, we must imagine Horace quite differently: as a Roman Socrates, no aristocrat by birth, but a man of intelligence and moral depth who tries to exploit a natural gift of irony to stir the conscience of others. To attain his goal, Horace set out to delimit the area occupied by Lucilian *libertas*. He avoided political topics, direct personal attacks of any sort, confessions about love affairs, mere anecdotes, in fact, all subjects which might tend to distort the image of himself which he desired to convey, all subjects which might interfere with the essential moral purpose of his Satires. It often seemed that Lucilius lost sight of his ethical end in his eagerness to denounce a personal enemy; but when Horace explores some fault, it is always obvious that he aims at the fault itself rather than at any particular person who may exemplify it.

In the First Book of his Satires, Horace openly criticized Lucilius and attempted to define the new features of his poetic *satura*. Lucilian freedom entailed moral irresponsibility at times, and also it incurred the charge of lacking artistic discipline. As an Augustan poet, Horace fulfilled the Classical ideals in many respects: his Satires exhibit that significant blend of poetic craftmanship and moral depth, of personal intimacy and personal restraint, of tolerance and ethical intensity.

When one comes from Horace and begins studying the Latin of Persius, one cannot miss the frequent verbal imitations of Horace's poems; indeed, I would not hesitate to claim that Persius knew the entire body of his predecessor's poetry by heart and must have pondered it constantly as he himself began to work on *satura*. Scholars have long since collected the passages which seem to owe much to an earlier line or lines of Horace; it would be easy to quote figures, as for instance that in Satire 5 more than fifty places seem reminiscent of Horatian lines. However, the reader of the translation must take this on authority; for him, it is more important to see how whole Satires of Horace—and, in some cases, of Lucilius—have suggested to Persius the general plan of his poems. Satire 1, which is so conscious of Lucilius and Horace, as we have seen, follows the general pattern of the Program Satire invented by Lucilius and improved by Horace. Satire 5, with its theme of moral liberty and assertion that all men but the wise are slaves, quickly reminds one of the ironic use of the same theme by Horace in *Serm.* II, 7. It would be virtually impossible to understand Persius without knowing Horace; and yet we must immediately add that Persius differs radically from his predecessor.

We may say, then, that Persius took over a poetic form which had reached its ideal Classical height in the Satires of Horace. The basic definition of *satura* remained unchanged, still permitting a wide variety of talents and moral attitudes: it continued to be hexameter poetry of personal moral criticism. Horace had increased the effectiveness of each element and disciplined the whole into poetic economy. By various ways he improved the plasticity of the hexameter, availed himself of Augustan enjambement and versatile rhythms, and made the verse both interesting and significant, a fundamental part of the poem's meaning. Among his other poetic improvements were verbal economy, avoidance of useless Hellenisms, insistence on wit that contributed to the poem rather than ridicule to conceal the absence of meaning. The *persona* of Horace lacks the variety and excitement of Lucilius; instead, we feel that we can trust our Roman Socrates to be impartial, to focus impersonally on the truth, without amusing himself or hurting others. Where Lucilius' morality often seemed suspect, it is safe to say that Horace made morality the essential quality of *satura,* drawing much closer to the philosophic schools than the aristocratic freedom of 120 B.C. would have permited. Because of their Socratic qualities Horace's Satires assume a permanent value that is absent from the work of his predecessor; he talks to all times, to everyone of us. No wonder that in a new age, when poetry was being encouraged again, a young man steeped in Horace and stirred by a different moral outlook as well as divergent artistic theories should set out to write the *satura* for his day.

We possess six Satires written by Persius, and the biography suggests that Persius died before bringing these to completion. Prior to these six poems in the manuscripts, as has been recently proved by the American scholar W. V. Clausen, there existed fourteen lines which are here entitled "Prologue to the Satires." These lines remain a source of controversy, even though their position can no longer be questioned. Some manuscripts assign to them the title of Prologue; others provide no title. It has been argued that they cannot be a prologue because they fail to make a point in specific reference to satire; hence, many regard the lines as a fragment of an unfinished poem irrelevant to the Satires but retained by Persius' editors at his death because of their poetic felicities. Others feel that the fourteen lines fall into two unconnected groups of seven lines apiece and that we have here two fragments of Persius' *juvenilia*. Some find the meter—choliambic instead of the regular dactylic hexameter—disturbing; while opponents point out that Phoenix of Colophon, a diatribal poet of the Third Century B.C., and possible prototype of Persius, characteristically wrote his moral denunciations in the choliambic meter. In my opinion, these lines do not constitute a successful or meaningful prologue. Persius sneers at the formal epic poets and expresses his own modest designs; then he ridicules the inept poets who write from false motives, namely, to earn a sizable profit. But there he stops, leaving it implicit that he himself claims different motives, that he is about to produce a type of poetry which is straight from the heart; but it is uncertain whether the poetry here implied is the *satura* which we subsequently meet. Nothing in this so-called Prologue conflicts with the material in Satire 1; but nothing in these choliambics really resembles the clarity of a Program Satire. Therefore, it might be safest to regard these lines as an incomplete fragment, possibly designed as a prologue if finished, but also quite possibly unrelated to the hexameter Satires which follow.

No definite criteria have ever been established for determining the order in which Persius wrote his poems, so I shall deal with them in the order in which they appear in the Manuscripts and our translation. Satire 1 functions as the traditional Program Satire; that is, it explains the satirist's conception of his poetic form in answer to a certain number of familiar objections. As we have already noted, Persius may well have started from Lucilius X in this poem. Lucilius, and Horace after him, had used dialogue to enhance the force of their ideas, creating an interlocutor who would voice objections against *satura*, thereby enabling them to state their satiric theories. Persius also creates an interlocutor (quite imaginary, to judge from the satirist's remarks in I, *44*) who attacks him immediately with the question: "Who'll read that sort of thing?" Persius dismisses the concern for a popular audience and counter-attacks, with an onslaught against the general literary public and the conventional poets and orators; this constitutes the major portion of the Satire. Although this general denunciation represents a negative program, it suggests the essential values of satire. To the satirist, the public and its favorites are corrupt, sensuous, materialistic, devoid of artistic and moral standards. Implicitly, then, Persius' poetry aims at different goals. He rejects mere popularity, mere mellifluousness, mere appeal to the jaded tastes of the court, and instead urges sound, well-reasoned matter, genuine poetry of the quality of the *Aeneid*. When the interlocutor hears this, he retorts with the traditional charge against satire: namely, that its program consists in personal attacks which, even though truthful, do nothing but hurt feelings. Again, Persius presents his program indirectly. He reviews the approaches of his predecessors, Lucilius and Horace, as I have already mentioned, and then deliberately places himself with them. However, just as Horace moderated the notorius "freedom" of Lucilius, so Persius suggests his own modification of Horace. He will, in a certain sense, mutter into his book; that is, he will not deal in personalities even as much as Horace. On the other hand, he starts from a different moral conception than Horace, whose "Golden Mean" and Socratic irony have long constituted the epitome of rational moderation. Where Horace assumed that each individual had faults which were perfectly corrigible, Persius denounces mankind: "There's not one of them who doesn't have ass's ears!" To sum it up, Persius here proclaims his program as follows: to deal unsparingly with the asininity of mankind (avoiding individual attacks) in a pungently direct style which will be the exact opposite of the sensuous nonsense emitted by the court poets.

Satire 2 starts from a particular situation, the birthday of Persius' dear friend Macrinus and the religious ceremonies of thanksgiving which are customary on such an occasion. Normally, the man celebrating his birthday would pour out a libation and make a prayer of thanksgiving for the year of happiness already granted him, then no doubt add a few personal requests, most frequently for long life and prosperity. In such prayers Persius finds his subject. Whereas Macrinus knows how to pray without demeaning himself or debasing the conception of divinity, others constantly involve themselves in blasphemy by their utterly materialistic view of life and of the gods. Here is a basic contrast, the essence of every Satire: in Satire 1 Persius opposed the court poets to himself as satirist, and now he opposes the crassly materialistic prayer to that of someone like Macrinus. It all amounts to the basic conception that mankind in general is hopelessly corrupt—just as it is asinine in its literary tastes—and only the wise man knows how to pray. Look at the others, he says, caught in their own inconsistencies: the fools who pretend to pray for a sound mind but really lust for an inheritance that presupposes the death of a wife or close relative; the superstitious old crone who prays that a newborn baby will make a prosperous marriage, only that; the fool who sacrifices his whole flock while praying for its increase. So it goes on, and the worst of it is that such people contaminate the divine ideal with their diseased conceptions. Confusing materialism for reality, they assume that the gods must of necessity epitomize the material approach to existence, "from our iniquitous flesh," as Persius admirably puts it, "deducing what would please the gods." There can be no doubt about the moral lesson in this succinct little poem: the true attitude of prayer, Persius concludes, depends upon possessing "a soul in harmony with the dictates of heaven, a mind pure in its secret places, a generous and honest heart." These are some of the most famous lines in the Satires, and they may well have influenced the similar conclusion of Juvenal's Tenth Satire: *orandum est ut sit mens sana in corpore sano* [". . . a sound mind in a sound body"].

Again in Satire 3 Persius begins with a concrete situation: it is late in the morning, and a young man, who should be studying, is still indulging lazily in sleep. Scholars do not entirely agree on how the satirist organized the scene, for Persius never makes the persons in his dialogues obvious. Some interpret this as a soliloquy, an internal discussion between the lazy and the conscientious parts of a man, quite possibly the satirist himself. Others find no evidence for such a view and prefer to believe that the young man protests against the criticism of a friend or tutor or ideal Stoic. In any case, Persius has set up his typical contrast between wisdom and folly, here specifically the opposition of serious study and immature self-indulgence. We hear of a number of sad examples of sloth and moral blindness, such as the tyrant (35 ff.), the malingering student (44 ff.), the ignorant centurion (77 ff.); until finally we concentrate on the fool who deceives himself into thinking that his illness, the result of his gluttony, is nothing and who brings on his death by further drinking. Indeed, Persius seems to be exploiting one of the common moral metaphors that equates physical with moral sickness. Horace had amused himself with the possibilities of the Stoic paradox in *Serm.* II, 3, and now Persius has given the paradox his interpretation: all men but the wise are "sick." The theme, which is implicit in the description of the tyrant and of the boy's pretended illness, emerges nakedly at the very center of the poem. "Check the ailment," advises the satirist, "before it's got to you and you won't have to sign away vast sums to the doctor." In other words, give your attention to genuine values, Stoic values, while you are young; otherwise, you will become so confirmed in your folly, like the tyrant, the centurion, and the self-deceiving invalid, that there will be no possible "cure."

Satire 4, like Satire 2, is another short poem, in fact the briefest of all the Satires. It also enjoys the dubious distinction of being the most obscene. This time, Persius finds his inspiration for an opening in one of the lesser Platonic dialogues, *Alcibiades I*. But where Plato represented the discussion between Alcibiades and his revered master Socrates as a serious inquiry into the possibilities of directing the destiny of a city-state without training, Persius assumes our familiarity with the situation and immediately focuses attention on the self-deception of Alcibiades. Socrates bears not the least resemblance to the Platonic figure nor to the Socratic ideal present in Horatian satire; instead, he becomes another Stoic wise man, the precise opposite and utter antagonist of the fool Alcibiades. Persius dismisses this dramatic framework midway through the poem, and, as he did in Satire 3, states his theme here in the center (*23-4*): "And none tries the descent into himself, no, not one!" Now, there can be no question but that the satirist drives towards the value of self-knowledge. He goes on to illustrate the fact that we can see most clearly the faults of others, hung, as the proverb has it, in a sack on their backs; but we utterly fail to perceive our own perversity. One who is sensuously luxurious can openly despise another's uncouth avarice, without being any better himself. Sometimes, indeed, one can impose upon others, to the extent that one receives general credit for virtues which one does not possess. To swallow such praise from the ignorant masses is the mark of a stupid man. Consider, says Persius at the end (*47* ff.) the typical faults of mankind, avarice, lust, and ambition: anybody who pursues these as though they constituted the goal of human life obviously does not know himself or the value of self-sufficiency. The Stoics idealize not the man exalted by the obsequious, brutal herd, but the man standing alone, confirmed in his wisdom by his own conscience. "Live in your own house," says the metaphorical satirist, "and learn what a bare lodging it is."

It is generally granted that Satire 5, the longest of the poems, is the finest. Like the previous Satires, it begins with a dramatic situation, a conversation between Persius and his beloved tutor and friend, Cornutus. The subject under discussion, seemingly rather tenuously connected with the theme later announced, concerns the influence which Cornutus has positively exerted on the young satirist and how Persius can honestly describe the enormous importance of Cornutus in his life. Should Persius give way to his emotions and launch into an epic panegyric of his tutor? Cornutus sharply rejects the idea and states a theory of style for Persius which reminds those familiar with Lucilius and Horace of the satirist's program: Persius must avoid highflown diction and stick to the simple ungarnished truth. "You stick to simple fare," says the tutor, borrowing a typical metaphor, one frequently appearing in Satire 1. At that, Persius proceeds to review his friendship with Cornutus: he tells how as an adolescent he ran the danger of wasting his talents, until he came under the care of Cornutus. Cornutus took charge and, like a craftsman of the soul, he constructed Persius' moral character to be the image of his own. Now they are united, two Stoics aiming at the identical goal: "some powerful affinity knits together our two lives." Persius has subjected himself to the single purpose of wisdom and in its service has found "freedom." No longer subordinate to his Master Cornutus, he lives with him as his friend and equal. Unity of purpose, uniformity of style, these represent Stoic values and form a clear contrast to the hundred false voices sought by the epic poets at the beginning of the Satire as well as to the thousand discordant ways of mankind in general, the topic immediately following (52 ff.). Thus, in the thematic contrast between unity and diversity, we can detect the symbolic function of the long opening section of the poem. Just as in Satire 4 the discussion between Socrates and Alcibiades dramatized the importance of self-knowledge, so here the conversation between Cornutus and Persius, Master and pupil also, dramatizes the virtue of moral freedom. These two, identical in their aims, will constitute the permanent pole of opposition to the series of moral slaves who will now occupy our attention.

Most men, far from making good use of their time and pursuing the one worthy end, involve themselves in variegated futilities such as typical avarice, luxury, and lust. What in fact we all desire—and here at last (*73* ff.) Persius openly states his theme, almost precisely in the center of the poem—is liberty, genuine moral liberty. It is automatic, however, for the Stoic to exploit the metaphor in liberty and develop his paradox, that all but the wise man are "slaves." Horace had exposed the fallacy of the paradox in *Serm.* II, *7;* Persius fully accepts the paradox as profound truth. He works his theme out in two directions. First, he takes the emancipated slave, proud of his legal freedom, and shows the difference between the mere title of freedom and genuine moral liberty (*73-131*). Then, he goes through the canonic faults, avarice, luxury, lust, ambition, and superstition, and reveals each one as a manifestation of "slavery." The final comment is ironic, confirming the thesis of Persius even as it denies it. A centurion, typically stupid as in III, *77* ff., sneers at the purveyor of such philosophy and, treating him as worse than a slave, refuses to buy a hundred such moralists—Greeks he contemptuously calls them—for a clipped coin. We have reverted to the theme of numeral diversity, but what a difference exists between the hundred mouths of the vapid poets and the hundred true Stoics. It is the centurion who is the slave, not those whom he ignorantly proposes buying.

If any extant poem of Persius remains unfinished, as the biography suggests, it would have to be Satire 6, whose conclusion many scholars consider to be abrupt and unsatisfactory. However, we can make good sense of it as it stands, so that we will not here indulge in conjecture. Suffice it to say that its structure differs considerably from that of the others; the reader may draw his own conclusions. The opening of the poem has an epistolary character, for Persius, writing from Luna (near modern La Spezia), addresses his good friend, the poet Caesius Bassus, at his retreat in the Sabine hills. It is nearly winter, and the two poets have withdrawn from Rome to the comforts of country villas. The introduction expresses the mood of contentment which the poet feels in his modestly comfortable surroundings; it reminds us of the satisfaction which Horace felt with his farm near Tibur. This modest happiness stands as the positive pole, to which is immediately contrasted the grasping discontent of the avaricious. And now the Satire becomes a dialogue between Persius and an assumed heir, as Bassus drops entirely out of consideration. Neither miserly nor luxurious, Persius voices his creed as follows (22 ff.): "As for me, I try to make the most of things." The heir protests at such principles and argues that Persius should never touch his capital, but always lay some aside and increase his wealth. Teasing the poor fool, Persius makes his first and only allusion to a Roman emperor, referring to the counterfeit triumph which Caligula ordered twenty years previously for his ignominious campaign against the Germans: he proposes to support this "triumph" lavishly. Naturally, the heir cannot protest now, not when Caligula's vicious ways are so familiar. Again,

Persius contemplates finding a different heir among the beggar herd near Bovillae, one less particular, less irritating than his natural heir, but conceivably related to himself in the distant past. The point is, his money belongs to him, to use as he desires, and the heir can make no legitimate claims on him to stint himself, not when he merely follows a moderate course of existence. As for the heir and his ilk, those who sell their souls for lucre can never attain the happiness of Persius.

What are the special qualities of Persius' poetry? In considering Persius we must examine both his poetic art and his moral approach.

The language of the satirist had traditionally been free of magniloquence, more likely to approach the direct, picturesque, but relaxed manner of everyday speech. Persius himself comments on the diction of his contemporaries among the court poets in Satire 1, making amply clear that he totally rejects verbiage which aims at the senses, not at the mind. Again, in Satire 5 he reveals a distaste for the counterfeit enthusiasm of the grand poet who requires a hundred mouths to say what might be expressed quite simply and honestly. However, if we were to conclude from these passages that Persius has adopted a style similar to that of Horace and Lucilius before him, we would be mistaken. While scrupulously avoiding the vapid grandeur of epic, our satirist creates for himself a unique style that has always provoked controversy. Basically, the argument may be put as follows: does Persius' style enhance his moral ideas, functioning as the necessary complement to them, or does this ingenious diction interfere with the statement of a simple, uncomplicated ethical system?

Direct and picturesque Persius is, but, because he abandons the relaxed informality of his predecessors, his directness and his picturesqueness take on an entirely new form. Glancing through his poetry, for instance, the reader will immediately observe how carefully each word has been chosen: the verbs carry special force; the adjectives have nothing trite about them, often serving metaphorically; where he can, the poet omits unessential words, especially the verb "to be"; if obscenity can help, he willingly adopts it. In short, Persius' language is among the most vigorous in Latin literature. A passage like I, 4 ff. illustrates this vigor perfectly. The sardonic note in "Dames of Unrelieved Virtue," the contempt in "dim-witted Rome," the image in the phrase about straightening corrupt scales, the rhetorical self-interruption as Persius hesitates to denounce current tastes, phrases like "grizzled heads" or "glum customs," details like those about playing marbles or growing long-faced and avuncular, and finally the long scene describing a poet's recitation and perversely rendering it as sexual intercourse between homosexuals: all this and more exists in the original Latin. Indeed, it would be no exaggeration to say that Persius' stylistic contrivances set the translator an impossible task.

When Greek and Latin writers commenced a poetic work, they usually set themselves a specific style which would conform to, and enhance, the ideas which they desired to express. Traditionally, the satirist had utilized the Plain Style because it most closely supported the *persona* of the satirist as a simple, unassuming, but intelligent and witty conversationalist. Persius violates the canons in his style: he is too direct and uncompromising to fit the Grand Style, yet at the same time he has forsaken simplicity in order to riot in a variety of studied phrases and conceits. The histories of Latin literature, which seem to have been written by men out of sympathy with the studied diction and poetic conceit nowadays so congenial to writers and critics alike, usually set Persius down as a special, but not very commendable, phenomenon in Latin. Following the lead of an erudite commentator named Johannes Lydus, of the Fifth Century A.D., they abandon Persius as quite hopeless and not worth the effort of comprehension, associating him with the Alexandrian poet Lycophron. Lycophron was the epitome of poetic obscurity throughout antiquity: he luxuriated in dark synonyms and periphrases in a lengthy poem called *Alexandra,* itself an obscure title, purporting to repeat the prophecies of Cassandra about the Fall of Troy and the future of the Trojans. I do not find the comparison between Persius and Lycophron valid, for Lycophron exploited a dramatic situation that justified obscurity—after all, Cassandra was doomed to make true prophecies which nobody would comprehend—and an Alexandrian taste for learned allusions; whereas Persius' studied language has no prototype in Roman satire, no analogue in the Latin literature of Nero's day, and dramatically conflicts with the role of simplicity which Persius seems to announce for himself both in Satires 1 and 5. However, it is useful to know one of the most common verdicts on Persius' style before trying to determine just how successful it can be with a sympathetic audience.

One way of looking at this matter is to compare Persius with his contemporaries among the court poets, at least from the point of view adopted by the poet in his Program Satire. After some space devoted to an indirect characterization of their ways, Persius proceeds in I, 93 ff. to quote the poetasters against themselves, first the clever devices which they use to end lines, then four complete lines of typical nonsense. It has even been suggested by some early commentators that he quotes the works of Nero himself, but we have no way of ascertaining the truth of the theory. In any case, as one reads the passage on the "Mimallonean bellowings," the prejudice of the satirist and his implicit stylistic purpose begin to take effect. Half the words are utterly superfluous, and to conceal this fact the poet has contrived to make them difficult. If we cut every adjective, we would do no damage to the basic picture of Dionysiac rites; what we would be doing is marring the mellifluous movement and the sensuous mood impressed upon the scene. Now, it is precisely this that Persius attacks and radically alters when he himself writes poetry. There is not a wasted word anywhere in his Satires; if anything, we would appreciate a few additional words to bridge over the ellipses and the compressed series of metaphors and other tropes. Furthermore, Persius has destroyed all empty music in the verse; he loves staccato rhythms, interrupted lines, avoids the enjambement which makes epic so moving, and, when he does rise to a crescendo, infuses the passion of moral fervor in what he says. In short, by contrast with the poetry which Persius quotes, his Satires achieve in their style the ideal by which to shock his day and drive directly to the heart of a moral problem. Finally, it is hardly necessary to note that our satirist scorns all such sensational subjects as Dionysiac rites, whose prime purpose would consist in arousing the prurient feelings of a corrupt generation. Far from "prostituting poetry"—and the metaphor is Persius'—to the perversity of the court, Persius sets out to attack that very perversity and demonstrate how disgusting it really is. For that he requires a style as far removed as possible from the operatic methods of his contemporaries.

Take the matter of obscenity, one of the marked characteristics of Persius' verse from Satire 1 on. Thanks to the translator's frankness, the reader now for the first time has the opportunity to discover this aspect of our satirist; no Victorian translator ever dared to render accurately the many places where specific remarks were made against an opponent's sexuality. But what is the purpose of Persius' directness? Horace had openly avoided any such theme or language, presumably because it tends to interfere with a rational perception of moral problems. However, when Persius writes, he considers the tastes of his own age, not an age of Classical discipline but one of Manneristic license; for him, the literary standards of Nero's court can best be rendered by an obscene metaphor: they amount to effeminacy, to homosexual self-indulgence. I need hardly mention the fact that homosexuality formed a regular part of the pleasures of Nero's circle, that the emperor himself acquired notoriety for "marrying" two of the prominent male performers of Rome, once in the role of the husband, once as the wife. To employ obscenity metaphorically or symbolically, as Persius does, means exploiting one of the most striking features of noble behavior in order to expose the full extent of corruption. For there is a connection between indulging in homosexuality and luxuriating in sensuous poetry on immoral subjects, at least for the moralist. Accordingly, Persius' obscenity constitutes the moralist's reaction to the mellifluous style, the sensational topics, and the generally perverse ways of the court poets and their patrons: it is harsh, makes the topic loathsome, and uses it ethically as the ideal symbol for the contemporary courtier.

If we were to search for the symbols with which the satirist surrounds himself, we would find that they almost universally involve the mental and mechanical processes; that is, while the ignorant and immoral are trapped by their own flesh, most strikingly of course by their sexual perversions, the satirist and the wise Stoics like him devote themselves to the true values of rational control. Accordingly, one of the first metaphors in Satire 1 utilizes the process of weighing, an important and difficult technique in those days, to define the virtue of accurate judgment as opposed to following the crowd. Turning to Satire 5, for example, we note that the description of Cornutus' influence upon Persius in 30 ff. abounds in images of this type: Cornutus is a sculptor, an architect, an artist who forms his product carefully. As for Persius, it would seem that he thinks of himself by preference as a "doctor," healing the sick souls of humanity. One of his favorite devices for rendering the moral corruption of others is to describe them as drunken, weighed down by excess food, sick, dying, especially in Satire 3, where the "sickness" of mankind constitutes the basic metaphor. When in Satire 1 the satirist's interlocutor criticizes him for his harsh manner, he puts it metaphorically: "But why harrow delicate ears with your cutting truths?" This grotesque picture, doubly effective by reason of its grotesqueness, refers to the current medical practice of cleaning out ears with a mild acid; Roman doctors used vinegar, whereas we often use a form of peroxide for a similar purpose. Persius aims to cleanse the ears of mankind and, through the ears, reach the reason and the soul. In v, *86* he introduces a Stoic speaker to expose the folly of Marcus Dama, the emancipated slave who boasts of his moral freedom; to many a reader it would seem at first sight ridiculous, but the fact is, Persius expects to win sympathy for the Stoic by appending a descriptive phrase: "his ears scoured with caustic vinegar." The man who himself has purified his ears, that is, his heart, can thereupon proceed to operate on others, using the acid of his tongue to shock his audience, to open their ears otherwise blocked to the voice of reason. It is in this sense that Cornutus talks to Persius earlier in the same Satire and uses the same medical metaphor as occurred in I, *107: radere* meaning "scrape" or "harrow." Persius has been trained like a doctor to scrape the sickly pale manners of his age, and for that he must employ direct language, not the false grandiloquence of the epic poets.

It should be fairly obvious by now that in concept Persius' style does complement his moral approach. He reacts against the effeminate diction of court poets and proceeds to speak directly and harshly, deliberately affronting the tastes of Neronian society by rendering its pleasures nauseating, contemptibly obscene, sickly. He is the doctor of souls, too concerned for the health of people to worry about their tender feelings, indeed convinced that health can only be attained by attacking these very feelings, the source of contemporary sickness. The gluttons among his audience—and this was one of the periods of the notorious Roman banquets—he constantly insults by exploiting the process of cooking and eating as metaphors for the soul; those who live for eating have obviously lost their souls and head for a moral death analogous to the gross end of most self-indulgent people. If we try to visualize the *persona* of the satirist, we picture a dedicated doctor or missionary, lean to the point of emaciation, unwittingly offensive by his fanatic ways, violent in his hatreds, utterly oblivious of human feelings, and afire with an ideal which somehow, to the cooler brains among us, lacks practicality.

Now, a harsh style contrasting so sharply with the effeminate diction of Neronian poets in general does have merits; its carefully chosen words, sparely used adjectives, totally economic diction, along with contrived phrases that somehow blend the goal of precision and the search for an allegorical significance, its abrupt transitions and open refusal to indulge in extensive dramatization all make their appeal to the mind, not the senses of the reader. He must work with this poetry, not sit back and let it flow meaninglessly but pleasantly over him. It is obvious that the satirist has labored over every word, and it is often necessary for the reader to repeat that labor in order to derive the allegorical significance within each successive phrase.

And yet, the more one exerts those rational responses which seem to be required by Persius' style, the more it becomes apparent that Persius has fundamentally failed to realize his goal. Whether his youth stood in his way or because he was incapable of translating Stoic doctrine into poetry, in any case the fact gradually emerges that the primary appeal of Persius' poetry is not to our mind but to our prejudices.

Persius says in I, *12:* "My wit has a mind of its own and makes me laugh." If one assumed from this that the satirist had adopted as his goal the same purpose as Horace, namely, laughingly to tell the truth, the Latin would quickly disabuse one: Horace's *ridere* can possess various connotations, but Persius' *cachinno* means but one thing, to laugh contemptuously and harshly. Thus, the ironic manner of Horace differs markedly from the sardonic attitude of the Stoic Persius; as Persius himself admitted, Horace persuaded his very victims to laugh with him at themselves, something which no reader of Persius ever does. Socratic irony does appeal to the reason, and in Horace's hands irony helps the reader to attain that Socratic ideal of self-knowlelge, for Horace admits his own fallibility and assumes it in others, without, however, despairing of the situation. True to the conviction of the Augustan Age, he firmly believes that men are basically rational and so can work out their salvation; he adopts the role of a teacher, slightly more advanced than his pupils, dedicated to the principle that we all can learn to live morally, hence happily. Laughter forms a necessary and pleasant part of this educational process.

Not so with Persius. Everything in his style and his manner, that is, his *persona,* tends to isolate him from the rest of us. He is the Stoic sage in his private paradise, from which he addresses us with his biting words, convinced, as he asserts in I, *121,* that we all have asses' ears. To argue from the premise that all men are fools except for the Stoics involves considerable distortion; still more serious, it tends to antagonize rather than convert the majority. Certainly some men would be shaken by the contempt of the satirist. Most, however, would feel themselves free of the faults imputed to them, or at least able to free themselves. And after all, the symbolic style of the satirist permits him to equate an ordinary human foible with something grotesquely unfair: a reluctant student becomes unformed clay by mere assertion, and a procrastinator becomes the rear axle of a pair of wheels. Instead of using similes or analogies having common points with the folly under discussion, Persius prefers the non-logical method of the metaphor and the symbolic scene. In short, he talks to his audience as though it were composed of Stoics able to comprehend his dogmas, or fools utterly beyond the reach of rational appeal. He never takes one concrete human fault and examines it in depth—for instance, materialism or ambition, as Horace might have done. Instead, he works from the symbolic-allegorical level; adopting some metaphorical theme, he shows how it can be applied to a variety of faults. When he ends, accordingly, the reader remains in possession of a symbol, often a powerful one, to be sure, but not a rational one. Persius' Satires assume a negative attitude: they denounce rather than instruct. Persius says of one poor fool, "You were born without a grain of sense (v, 119)"; for such a man, the satirist offers no hope.

Possibly we might accept the black picture of humanity if we could be sure of the satirist's own wisdom, but Persius does not strike most readers as sufficiently experienced. Compared with Seneca, for all the latter's compromises, Persius is a lost child. Seneca's letters abound in scenes closely observed, filled with exact details noted down by the writer in person; Persius' Satires reflect no such minute observation. One would never realize, for example, the political crisis in Rome or the militant opposition assumed by some Stoics; nor does the economic or social crisis emerge with any clarity. Many examples Persius has drawn not from observation but from his readings, re-working Horace, Lucilius, Terence, and his Stoic sources. Even his picture of Neronian literature, depending indubitably on his own observations, is marred by inaccuracy. Where do Seneca, Lucan, and Petronius fit into this scheme? Perhaps it is true that Persius is interested in the timeless rather than the contemporary, but he must make his statement to his own generation. His generation, like those that have succeeded him, must have judged him essentially as a bookish moralist, well-read but not very profound, a clever stylist rather than a great Stoic satirist.

Although we must rank Persius below both Horace and Juvenal as a satirist and although he lacks the scope and human understanding of contemporaries like Seneca, Persius' work has unique features that justify considerable study. First, he is the only Stoic satirist, among a group of poets who preferred an eclectic type of morality. While he has not succeeded in giving his Satires that spark of inspiration which suffuses the work of the Epicurean poet Lucretius, his severe morality and harsh antagonism against foolish mankind originate as much in Stoicism as in the personality of the satirist; and the question might occur whether such a brand of Stoicism could ever stimulate effective satire. Secondly, Persius stands unique among surviving writers of his period for his uncompromising opposition to the prevailing corruption in court circles. The great writers of the Neronian Age are Seneca, Petronius and Lucan, all of whom lived lives of compromise and wrote literature that incorporates to some extent this spirit of compromise. When we read Persius, we meet at last the hard resistance of a man who knows Nero's court well and utterly refuses to be taken in by its meretricious attractions. Thus, Persius represents an otherwise unknown group of Stoics and men of principles who hated Nero and eventually found in Vespasian a ruler able to promote their ideal for Rome. But perhaps the most unique feature remains the one least likely to emerge in translation: namely, Persius' Latin style. The Stoics can claim no credit for this feature; it is all Persius'. Not only was he unique in his generation—something he apparently desired to be, in order to define his reaction against the "effeminate" poetic style of his contemporaries—but he continued to be unique throughout the succeeding centuries of Latin literature. In the end, he could be compared only with the unique (and truly obscure) Hellenistic poet Lycophron.

This new translation by W. S. Merwin brings out the precision of Persius' language and makes it patent how carefully Persius selected his words; it makes his compressed phrases and curious conceits more lucid, thus rendering comprehensible what in the Latin strikes the reader at first as decidedly obscure. It is one of the great tragedies of Roman literature that Persius, like his contemporary Lucan, did not live long enough to attain a mature style that might capably sustain his moral vision. As it is, we read Persius' style as unique and as one which might have become uniquely great.

The unusual aspects of Persius' Satires provoked controversy even during his lifetime. The Biography tells us one story of their effect. After the satirist had completed one recitation, the young Lucan was heard to remark: "That is real poetry, whereas all that I have written is utter tripe, child's play!" As a result of Persius' influence, it is often conjectured, Lucan turned away from trivial court poetry and began his Stoic epic. We need hardly wonder how the more frivolous members of the court circle received these harsh, unmusical Satires: they would undoubtedly have ridiculed Persius as a child and paid scant attention to his attacks. Whether or not there were allusions to Nero in Satire 1 and elsewhere—and scholars will probably always disagree on this point—the fact remains that Nero took no overt notice and Persius was primarily a poet of and for the small band of Stoics opposing the current of Roman history.

After Persius' premature death, his Satires and other poetic works came into the hands of his beloved tutor Cornutus; the Satires were unfinished, and the other works were so immature as to be not worth saving. Cornutus discussed the matter with Persius' mother and wisely persuaded her to suppress all but the Satires. In their unfinished condition, these latter required editorial labor, which another of Persius' former friends, the eminent lyric poet mentioned in Satire 6, Caesius Bassus, willingly assumed. The Biography tells us that a number of verses were dropped from one poem, which poem we do not know. Otherwise, it is difficult to estimate the editorial achievement of Bassus. Because the tendency of ancient editors seems to have been to remain closely faithful to the original text, scholars estimate that we now possess the Satires essentially as Persius wrote them. As soon as the little volume appeared, literary controversy erupted: the Biography states that men immediately took sides and either praised the poetry or tried to tear it apart. A generation later, interest in Persius still continued unabated. Martial, writing in the 90's, produced an epigram in which he favorably compared the terse economy of the Satires with the long-winded nonsense of a popular epic poet; precisely the type of recognition which the dead poet would have appreciated. Martial's contemporary, Quintilian, knew Persius' works well and cited him carefully, even commenting on the rare form of one of his words; an indication that the scholars had already commenced their seemingly endless task of explicating the satirist. Finally, the Biography stems from this same period of the 90's, a generation after Persius' death, and attests to the fact that the scholars found much in Persius to inspire them. A decade later, Juvenal started publishing his Satires. Few scholars would hesitate to affirm that Juvenal knew the work of Persius, profited by his predecessor's mistakes, and alluded to Persius' poems.

When studying other Latin poets, with the exception of such immediate and eternal favorites as Vergil and Horace, the student invariably finds that he cannot trace the manuscript tradition of the poet back beyond a certain period, usually in the Fourth Century A.D. Persius' Satires belong to the smaller class of works which remained in constant circulation throughout antiquity; our present text depends upon manuscripts whose affiliations can be followed with confidence back to that first posthumous edition produced by Caesius Bassus. Persius won wide distribution for the same reason that he provoked controversy: because he was a difficult poet with a unique style and a healthy moral tendency. By the end of the Second Century A.D. and throughout the next two centuries, the creative spirit had gone out of Latin literature, and writers were occupied in repeating and varying the inventions of their eminent predecessors, with great versatility, true, but without vital significance. Persius struck the tastes of this period admirably. His Satires became a school text forced down the throat of unwilling young boys. Scholars and moralists appropriated the Satires; poets received no inspiration from them. What satire there was assumed the severe, but much more lucid, form of the Juvenalian or Lucilian attack, far from the ingenious but somehow self-contradictory obscurities of Persius.

The young emperor of the early Third Century, Alexander Severus, who had more than the usual share of moralistic education, used to quote reverently II, *69;* "dicite, pontifices, in sancto quid facit aurum?" ["As for you, priests, there's one thing I wish / You'd explain. What's gold doing in the sanctuary?" Translation by Merwin]. And we find that throughout the next two centuries the men who refer to Persius belong in one of the two groups, either in the class of school teachers and commentators or in the new set of Christian theologians and Church fathers, whose purpose was somehow to interpret Christian principles to a world steeped in pagan Classical literature and philosophy. We need say nothing more about the commentators, who delighted in a difficult poet, but who also have given us many of the interpretations upon which we still base our understanding of certain portions of the Satires. Among the Church fathers, the one who knew Persius best and quoted him most freely was Jerome, a fine scholar in his own right. It is not difficult to see why the Satires appealed to a Christian apologist: they stem from the very age in which Christianity began, and they thoroughly condemn the pagan environment which Christianity set out to change. The rigidity of the Stoic position commended itself to many Christians, who often attacked Classical culture with the very words used by the Cynic-Stoic preachers before them. Thus, for Augustine in *The City of God* II, *6,* the passage in Satire III, *66-72* could be generally applied to the moral sickness of the pagan world:

> discite et, o miseri, causas cognoscite rerum:
> quid sumus et quidnam victuri gignimur, ordo
> quis datus, aut metae qua mollis flexus et unde,

quis modus argento, quid fas optare, quid asper
utile nummus habet, patriae carisque propinquis
quantum elargiri deceat, quem te deus esse
iussit et humana qua parte locatus es in re.

[Oh wretches, come learn the causes of things—what we are,
What manner of life we were born for, to what station
Brought forth, how and when to ease round the turning point, and
The limitations of wealth, what it's right to wish for,
The uses of new-minted coin, how much should be spent
On your relatives, how much on your country, to what
Calling God has summoned you, and what your position is
In human affairs.

TRANSLATION BY W. S. MERWIN.]

Whether or not Persius would have appreciated the trend of his popularity, we cannot really say; but it seems significant that his Satires exerted their influence as isolated passages rather than integrated poems, to be dissected by the commentators, studied by the lexicographers, and cited out of context by Christian apologists.

Interest in Persius never died out. The manuscript tradition continued unbroken through the Dark Ages on to the Carolingian Renaissance, after which Persius' Satires constituted a regular part of the curriculum. Our earliest complete manuscript, from Montpellier in France, comes from this period in the Ninth Century; and the large number of manuscripts which Clausen has recently collated from this same general time, attest to a widespread acquaintance with our satirist. The Satires were among the earliest printed works, the first edition appearing in Rome in 1470. There have been many translations, nearly sixty, it has been reckoned. Such translations, as for instance the well-known one by Conington in English, have generally incurred the criticism that they have been produced by Latinists rather than poets. It is to be hoped that the present version, achieved by a young poet sympathetic with his material, will succeed in presenting one of Rome's most ingenious and personally enthusiastic poets to the modern mind. In many respects Persius' virtuosity, coupled as it is with such passion, can say more to us and our literary sensibilities than it could to many an age before our time.

W. S. ANDERSON

Prologue

PROLOGUE TO THE SATIRES

At no time have I sluiced my mouth in the Fountain
Of Hippocrene, nor (if my memory serves me)
Have I dreamed ever on two-peaked Parnassus, that I
Should burst forth this way, without warning, a poet.
I leave to them whose busts the fawning ivy
Favors all claim to the Muses of Helicon
And the spring at Pirene which imparts pallor: not more
Than half a member of their clan, I offer my song
At the bards' banquet. Who loosened the parrot's
Racketing tongue and got the magpie to talk
But that master of arts, that disburser of genius,
And incomparable ventriloquist: The Belly.
Flash these crow-poets and magpie-poetizing
Females one glimpse of the ready cash, and you'd swear
The Muses' nectar was no sweeter than their song.

Satire One

PERSIUS

"Oh mortal ambition, oh towering emptiness
Of human enterprise . . ."

THE OTHER

Who'll read that sort of thing?

PERSIUS

Are you asking me? No one, by Hercules.

THE OTHER

No one?

PERSIUS

At most one or two.

THE OTHER

Lamentable and disgraceful!

PERSIUS

Why? Are you sad that our Dames of Unrelieved Virtue
Prefer Labeo? Spare yourself. Let dim-witted Rome
Disparage at pleasure; why appoint yourself to straighten
Her shamelessly crooked scales? Stick to your own judgment.
For there's not a soul in the place who—oh if only I

Could tell the secret—well, and I must tell it, what with
These grizzled heads of ours and our glum customs coming
To mind, in fact all that we've busied ourselves with
Since we left off playing marbles and grew long-faced
And avuncular. So, please, your forgiveness. For I can't
Help myself. My wit has a mind of its own and makes me
Laugh.
Locked in, we get down to it—verse, prose, something
Grand, making uncommon demands on the breath.
And in due course you'll favor the crowd with it, out of
A raised chair, in a new white robe, groomed to a hair,
Your throat loosened with syrup, a birthday sardonyx
Large in your gestures, and your eye, every so often,
Letting them in on it. Then, as the deft phrases
Find the way to their loins and stroke them within there,
You'll see the hefty sons of Rome's best families roused
Not in a nice way: quivering, and their words not edifying.
Dirty old thing, concocting temptations for the ears
Of others, now that you're poxed, shrivelled, and past it!

THE OTHER

And what good's your knowledge if your inner ferment, that
Wild fig tree, born in you, never bursts from your breast?

PERSIUS

We're white
And senile with study. Oh shame on you! Is all your
Learning nothing to you unless people know about it?

THE OTHER

But it's delicious when they point and say, "That's him." And
To have a hundred unkempt schoolboys worrying over
Your text, really, wouldn't you like it?

PERSIUS

See, Romulus' sons,
Glutted with food, inquire over their cups, "Now what has
Divine poetry to offer?" And at this point there's always
A character in a purple cloak to lisp and whine
A rancid number about Phyllis, Hypsipyle, or
Some such elevated and chop-fallen rot, making it
Melt word by word in his mouth. The others appreciate it:
"How happy," they say, "Your poet's ashes must be
At this moment. You'll have made the grave-stone seem
positively
Light over his bones." From the head of the table this; at
Its foot they agree that his tomb and blessed ashes
Cannot fail to produce violets.

THE OTHER

You laugh, and you
Turn up your hooked nose too often. Would you have me
believe
That any man whose writings seemed worth the cedar oil
To save them from moths is above hankering after
Men's mention for such an issue of songs as need have
No fear that they'll end up wrapping mackerel or twisted
Around a pinch of frankincense?

PERSIUS

Whoever you are
Whom I've made up to argue with, if at any time
I should write something fine (it would be a rare bird,
of course),
Something felicitous, I'm not one to shy away
From praise. I'm not constructed of horn. Only don't expect me

To agree that your cries of "Bravo" and "Exquisite"
Constitute some final criterion. Consider
What else is called "Exquisite": Labeo's drunken Iliad,
The lovelorn compositions which the gentry declaim
After heavy dinners, and for that matter the verses scrawled
By sprawlers on citron-wood couches. You're an old hand
At dishing up hot tripe and palming off a rattled client
With an old cloak, and yet, "Truth," as you put it, "is my
Love, tell me the truth about myself." How could one?
Do you want me to try? You bald ninny with your bulbous
Stomach sagging a good half yard ahead of you. Oh
Fore-and-aft-facing Janus, whom no needling stork
Can sneak up on, whom no hand can make fun of, mimicking
Ass's ears, at whom no tongue can be stuck out like some
Apulian hound's with a thirst on him! As for you,
Gentlemen with the pedigrees, who must get along
Without eyes in the backs of your heads, you'd do as well
To face the irreverent performances behind you.
What do people say?

THE OTHER

They say, "Now at last there are
Soft songs and verses flowing so smoothly that a nail
Could slither over their polish and not find the joints.
The poet gets his lines as straight as though he'd surveyed them;
Whether he writes of morals, luxury, or the luncheons
Of kings, the Muse sees to it that he hits it off
In the grand manner."

PERSIUS

That's how we come to have
Heroics haled forth by habitual dabblers

In Greek, whose whole art is not up to describing
A few trees or extolling the country life—its plenty,
Its paniers and hearths, the hay-piles smoking for
The feast of Palilia, and out of them stepping
Remus, and you, Cincinnatus, with your polished
Plow-share, and your flustered wife coming to robe you
Dictator, while the oxen look on; the lictor
Will drive home your plow . . . Ah, that's exquisite, poet!
One buries his nose in the dessicated pages
Of Bacchanalian Accius; and there exist some who
Can't tear themselves away from Pacuvius' warty
Antiope and "her dismal heart propped up with woes."
And when you see bleary fathers stuffing their sons with
This sort of instruction, do you wonder how the latter
Come to gabble such a goulash of language? And can't you
Guess the origin of those mincing lyrics which give
The seated gentry such pleasure?

Aren't you ashamed
That you can't save some old geezer's bacon without wanting
A pat on the back? "You're a thief," someone announces
To Pedius. For answer he juggles the charges
Into elegant antitheses, and is applauded
For his high-toned figures of speech: "Why, it's beautiful!"
Beautiful? Romulus, does that really send you? Maybe
You're not the man you used to be. Do you think I'm likely
To snivel and fish out a coin because some ship-wrecked
Individual belabors us with a song, meanwhile
Holding up a picture of himself adrift on a bit
Of ship's timber? No, tell him if he wants to dissolve me
With his sad story, it takes real tears, not salt water
Which someone's been up all night preparing.

THE OTHER

Well, anyway
There's elegance in the recent verse, and suavity
Instead of the crude old style. When you think how they
manage
To round out a line with "Berecynthian Attis,"
Or, "the dolphin then clove cerulean Nereus," or
Thus, "from the long Appenines we borrow a rib."

PERSIUS

Oh arms
And the man! What have we here but bubbles, and the sort
Of swollen bark under which you find the old bough
Shrivelled up to nothing? Now let's have something tender,
To be recited with a limp neck.

THE OTHER

"They filled their fierce horns
With Mimallonean bellowings." Or, "The Bassarid,
About to rip the head from the gambolling calf," or
Again, "The Maenad, ready to rein in the lynx
With braids of ivy, redoubles the Dionysian
Cry, and reverberant Echo returns it."

PERSIUS

Do you think
Stuff like that would get written if our generation
Hadn't been born without balls? Maenads! Attis! Watery
Saliva slopping around on the lips with the rest
Of the spit! No sign there of a table pummelled
For the one word, and nails bitten to the quick.

THE OTHER

But why
Harrow delicate ears with your cutting truths? You know,

You're likely to find the doorsteps of the great
Chilly, and—listen—there's the snarl of the dog.

PERSIUS

All right, as
Far as I'm concerned, from now on everything's white. Bravo!
Everybody's nice, everybody's incomparably
Wonderful! Now are you happy? "Please," you say, "do not
make
A smell here." So paint a couple of snakes upon the wall
To say, "Boys, the place is sacrosanct: do your pissing
Elsewhere." I'm off, myself.

And yet Lucilius took
The skin off this city; he flayed you, Lupus, and you,
Mucius, and ground you till his molars broke. And sly Horace
Could tease his way into the guts of his laughing friend
And touch the fault there; he had a trick of sticking out
His nose and hanging people on it. And I mustn't
Mutter a word? Not to myself? Not into a ditch? Not
Anywhere? Well, I will. I'll bury it here. Little book,
I've seen this, seen it. *There's not one of them who doesn't*
Have ass's ears! And this secret, this diminutive
Joke of mine I wouldn't swap for all your Iliads.

You that have been fanned by the fire-eating breath
Of Cratinus, oh you that have grown pale with poring
Over Aristophanes and the rage of Eupolis,
If your taste runs to such diet, glance at these lines.
For I hope for a reader whom those authors have
Kindled and purified. I can forgo the sort
That gets a kick out of laughing at Greek slippers and
Nearly splits with the humor of shouting, "Hey One-Eye!"
At one-eyed men. And I can get along without, say,

The hick magistrate who's so impressed with himself
For having put down short pint measures somewhere
In the benighted provinces, that he's convinced
He's an ornament to the empire. As for the card
Who finds the sight of an arithmetical computation
Or a geometrician's figures traced in the sand
Inexpressibly funny, and that other who's ready
To dissolve into guffaws if some little skirt plucks
A Cynic by the beard, I'm delighted to forfeit
Their attentions. Let them go spell out
The playbills plastered up in the Forum, for
Their morning reading. And the maundering phrases
Of Calliroe are good enough for their afternoons.

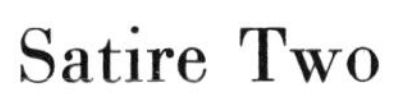

Satire Two

Set a white stone, Macrinus, against this day which marks
In the lapse of your years another ended. And pour out
To your Genius the unmixed wine. You're not one of those
Who bargain in their prayers—such bargains in such prayers
that
The gods themselves have to be taken to one side
To hear them. So many of our best citizens feel
The need to seal up their offerings in incense pots
Which breathe no secrets. It's not everyone who'd be willing
To have mutterings and low whispers forbidden in
The temples, and few could be open about everything
They apply for. Oh yes, they pitch up their voices (and
In the hearing of strangers) to request "a sound mind,
Good reputation, reliable conscience"—adding
Under their breath, for nobody's benefit
But their own, "Please let my uncle cash in his chips, I'll give
him
A rousing send-off," or, "Hercules, patron of windfalls,
Kindly let my hoe turn up a crock full of silver
And please remove my ward, who stands between me and
The inheritance; after all he's one solid scab

From head to foot, puffy with acrid bile, and there's
Nerius burying his third wife." Do you slosh your head
In Tiber twice and three times of a morning and there
Sluice off the night's leavings, just so you can go
Through all the holy motions and send up prayers like these?
I've one question. It's not much to ask. How do you feel
About Jupiter? I mean, would you place him above—
"Above whom?" Well, say above Staius; is anything
Wrong with him, for a choice? Name me a more punctilious
Judge, or more suitable guardian for an orphan.
Well, this same prayer, now, with which you'd planned to
solicit
The attention of Jove, go repeat it to Staius.
You'll hear him exclaim, "Holy Jupiter!", and not just
The once. And do you think Jupiter will be able
To hear you without taking his own name in vain?
Just because when it's thundery the fire from heaven
Blasts an oak instead of your roof-tree, maybe you think
That your peccadillos have been overlooked. And because
You're not lying out in a little enclosure (Victim
Of Lightning: Avoid) under the combined auspices
Usual in such cases—an Etruscan witch
And the sacrificed guts of a two-year-old sheep—do you
Think it follows that Jupiter will allow you
To pluck out his insensitive beard in handfuls? And what
Have you bestowed upon the gods, that they're so willing
To indulge you? Those little favors of greasy offal?
Watch granny (or aunty), fearful of the gods, lift
Baby out of his cradle and—a great one at fending off
The evil eye—with her middle finger smear
His forehead and his drooling lips with her charmed spit, then

Rock that shrivelled Hope in her arms, her prayers collaring
The estates of Licinus for him one minute, the mansions
Of Crassus, the next. "And may kings and queens pick him
For a son-in-law and the girls fight over him and
Roses pop up in his footsteps!" May no prayer of mine
Ever be mouthed by a nurse! Refuse her, I beg you,
Jupiter, though she puts on a white dress to pray in!

You petition for sound limbs and a body which will answer
Even in age. Good. But then those mountainous platters,
Course after rich course, compel the gods to ignore your
Prayer, and forbid the compliance of Jupiter.

Itching for wealth, you slit a bullock's throat, and
With the guts invoke Mercury: "Let my household gods
Contrive fortune for me, my flocks and herds multiply."
And how will they manage that, half-wit, if the fat
Of your beasts, one after the other, is rendered
In the flames? But he keeps slogging away with his entrails
And fatty pasties, determined to get rich: "This one
Means more and more fields, this one more flocks, and this one
Is a lot more, then this one, and this one . . ." till
His sigh at finding himself with no more hopes, no more
Money, nothing but his disappointment.

If I regaled you with silver wine bowls crusted thick
With gold your heart would thump, you'd go damp with pleasure,
Sweat would drip from your left breast. No wonder you think
The gods' faces ought to be gilded; you assume they'd
Be proud of it. You say, "Let's set at the head of this
Bronze brotherhood the one who sends us the nicest
Dreams, and none of the sticky kind. Let's give him
A gold beard." So much for Numa's earthenware, and
The bronze vessels of Saturn; so much for

The water jars of the Vestals, and the Tuscan
Crockery. They've all been replaced by gold.
Oh souls hunched low, with thoughts empty of heaven, what
Point is there in filling the temples, too, with our ways,
And from our iniquitous flesh deducing
What would please the gods? It's the flesh, you know, which has
Polluted our olive oil with cassia, and made nonsense
Of the Tyrian purple, using it to steep fleeces
From Calabria. It's made us grub in shells after
Pearls and root shiny ore out of the ground. It does
Wrong, and again wrong, and yet grows rich by its own
Degradation. As for you, priests, there's one thing I wish
You'd explain. What's gold doing in the sanctuary?
I should think it's about as much use to the gods as
Those dolls which virgins present to Venus. We'd do better
To bring to the altar what no bleary scion
Of great Messala can afford on his magnificent
Salver, namely, a soul in harmony with the dictates
Of heaven, a mind pure in its secret places,
A generous and honest heart. Grant me these to dedicate
In the temples and over plain bread I shall offer up thanks.

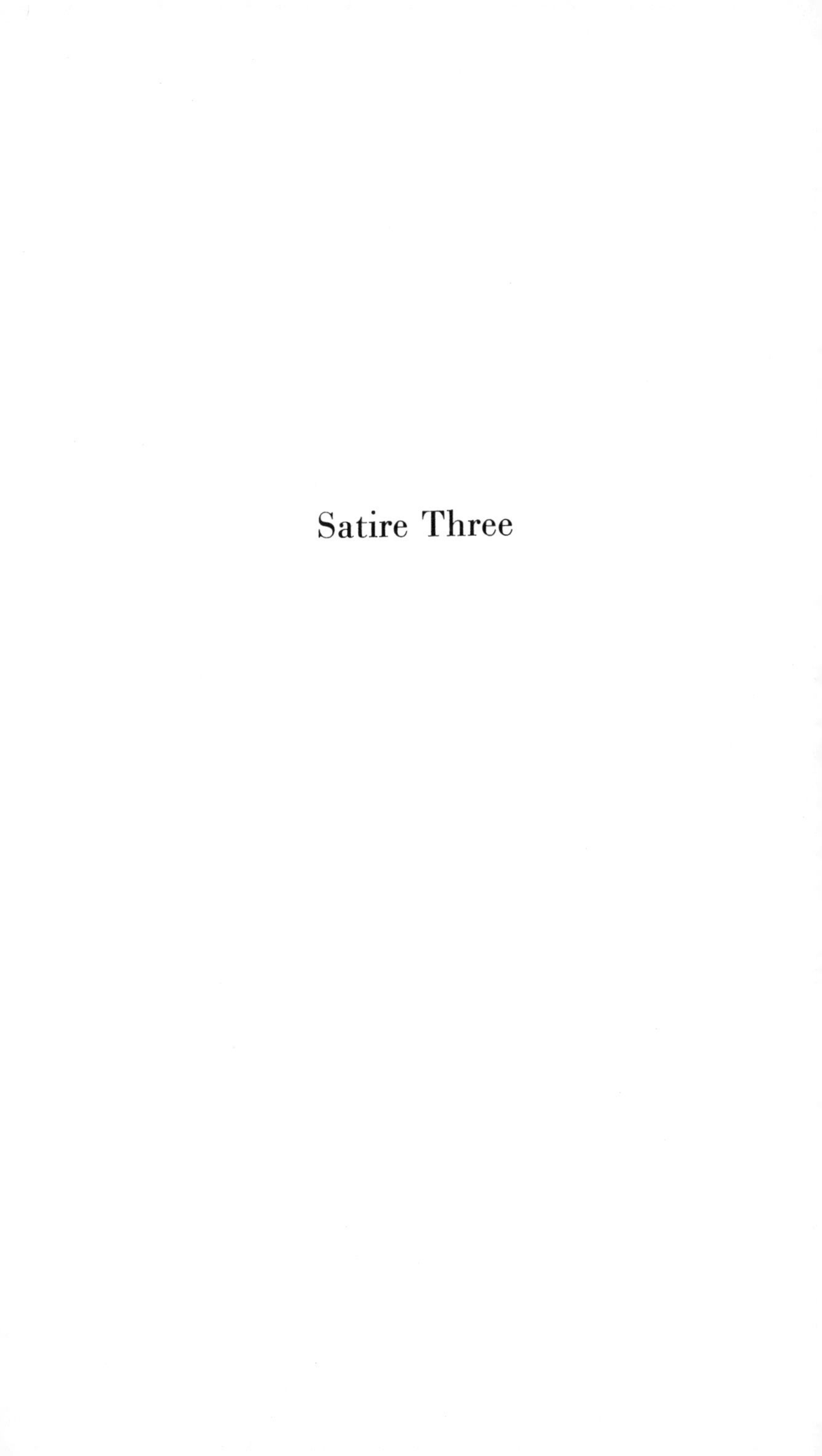

Satire Three

"Aren't you ever going to get up? There's the morning light
Getting in at your window, jimmying the cracks. And if we'd
Been plastered on Falernian last night, surely we could have
Snored it off by this time, when the shadow's at the fifth
Mark on the dial? Well, what have you in mind? The mad
  Dog-Star
Has been parching the dry harvest for some time now, and
The cattle are under the broad elms . . ." it's a friend talking.
Whereupon: "You don't mean it! Really? Oh, somebody
Come this minute! Is the house empty?" He's bursting
With vitreous bile and he bawls, "I'm splitting," till you'd swear
It was all the asses in Arcadia braying.
Then the book is snatched up, the hairless parchment in two
  colors,
Paper, jointed reed-pen—and then the whining starts: the
Ink's too thick, it sticks to the pen, then when it's watered
It's not black enough, and it splatters.

Idiot, getting
More idiotic by the day, have we really come
To this? Go on: fuss like some coddled dove or rich man's
Infant that insists on its food being sieved for it
And has tantrums at the sound of a lullaby.

"But how
Can I write with a pen like this?" And who do you think
You're fooling with those excuses tuned in the minor?
It's you yourself that's at stake, and you're drifting into
Imbecility; it's contemptible. Consider
A jug potted from cheap clay and poorly fired; it will ring
False when you strike it, and betray its flaw. As for you,
you're
Soft, you're wet (to continue the image), you ought to be
Grabbed before you're a minute older, and licked
Tirelessly into shape on a fast wheel. But you've got
The family acres, wheat enough to get by on,
You can display to your household gods an immaculate
Salt-cellar, and for the rites of the hearth you know
Where the next offering's coming from. So why worry?
But does that really satisfy you? Are you quite happy
Till you've puffed yourself up fit to split because you're
A descendant (number one thousand) of some Tuscan
Ancestor, and parade once a year with the gentry,
In purple, to salute your censor? Oh throw your
Baubles to the crowd! I know you outside and in,
And I wonder—does shame have no hold on you? You're
heading
For habits as slack as loose-living Natta's, with his
Wits vice-rotted, every organ imbedded
In fat, and himself beyond any notion
Of wrong, of what he's lost, sunk so deep that he doesn't
Even send up a bubble!

Great father of the gods, upon
Raging tyrants whose brains, tainted with the venom
Of ruinous lust, are turned by it, oh visit

No punishment but this: let them behold Virtue
And die of the knowledge that they have lost her! Never
Did the bronze bull of Sicily, roasting its victims, roar
With more horrible torments, nor did sword
Ever waken such terror, swinging from the gilded panels
Of a ceiling over the purple necks beneath,
As the torments and terror with which a man beholds
The abyss open and says to himself, "I'm falling," and
His liver goes lily-white, and the wretch can't even tell
His wife about it.

I remember, when I was a boy
I used to make my eyes bleary with olive oil, rather
Than have to declaim Cato's grandiloquent death-speech (that
Delight of my feeble-minded preceptor, a piece
Which my father would drag his friends in to hear, and then
drip
With joy as he listened). Wasn't I right? For at that time
All I cared about was what I could rake in if
The dice turned up high sixes, or lose on a low throw,
And not being foxed, at pebble-toss, by the small throat
Of the jar, nor worsted at whipping the boxwood top.

But you're over your ignorance now: you can sort out
What's straight from what isn't; your education
Favored the doctrines of the learned Porch that's daubed
All over with Medes in breeches; you've been pumped full of
Philosophy—and the Stoic persuasion, at that,
Which young men with shaved heads, nourished on husks and
big plates
Of barley gruel, and short on sleep, night after night
Pore over; Pythagoras' Letter Of Life has made
Plain to you how it branches, with the steep road on the right,

And still you're snoring? Still wobble-headed and slack-jawed,
Yawning like a box, and limp, after yesterday's
Debauch? Had you hoped to get anywhere? Were you
Aiming your bow at anything in particular?
Or do you just fling brick-bats and rubble after
Any old crow, and go where your feet prefer, drifting
From moment to moment?

It's no use fussing for a dose
Of hellebore when the skin's already puffed up
And sickly; check the ailment before it's got to you
And you won't have to sign away vast sums to the doctor.
Oh wretches, come learn the causes of things—what we are,
What manner of life we were born for, to what station
Brought forth, how and when to ease round the turning point,
and
The limitations of wealth, what it's right to wish for,
The uses of new-minted coin, how much should be spent
On your relatives, how much on your country, to what
Calling God has summoned you, and what your position is
In human affairs. Get these straight, and don't envy
Some character because his cellar's so crammed with food from
Bulging Umbrians whose cases he's taken that the stuff
Stinks in corners, along with pepper and gammons,
Souvenirs of Marsian clients—or because his
First keg of sardines isn't empty.

At this point
You can count on some goat-odored centurion to
Butt in with, "I know what I know and that's good enough
For me. I don't hanker to be an Arcesilaus
Or some old limp-necked wreck of a Solon with
Eyes glued to the ground, mouth working away mumbling

To himself like a dog with the rabies, and his words
Balancing on his jutting lip as he mulls over
The dreams of who knows what prostrate old wheeze, about
how
Nothing can be born out of nothing, and nothing into
Nothing can return. And you grow pale over pronouncements
Like this? You give up a good dinner for them?" Whereupon
The crowd positively splits and, wrinkling his nose, our
Muscular lad goes off into billowing guffaws.

Then there's this case who says to his doctor, "Examine me,
I've this funny fluttering in my chest, there's something
The matter with my throat, and my breath's bad; please
Have a good look." So he's told to rest, but after three nights
(The blood behaving more soberly in his veins)
He hales a thirsty moderate-sized jar to a friend
Who's comfortably off: could he have some vintage Surrentine,
Please, just now before he takes his bath? "You're looking pale,
Old fellow." "It's nothing." "I'd keep an eye on it,
Whatever it is: you're sallow, and you may not
Have noticed it, but look how you're swelling." "Your color's
worse
Than mine. Don't try that tutor act on me, I attended
My Tutor's funeral ages ago. But you're still here." "Forget
I mentioned it! I won't again!" So, wadded with dinner till
His stiff belly's white, with a steady eructation
Of sulphurous marsh-gas wafting from his gullet,
He goes to be bathed. Where a fit of the shakes catches him
Sozzling, knocks the hot tumbler out of his hand; his
Bared teeth chatter, and little chunks of meat, still running
With gravy, slither from his loosened lips. Then come trumpet
And torches, and our fine friend, daubed thick all over

With ointments (for the aroma) and laid out on
A high bed, presents his stiff heels to the door. And
Yesterday's freedmen (sporting liberty caps to prove it)
Cart him off.

"All right, stupid, take my pulse; come on,
Put your hand on my heart. I haven't any fever.
Feel my hands and my feet. They're not cold." I'd like to follow
The results if your eyes lit on a bit of cash
Or if that little dish next door were to slip you
A nice smile. Heart still steady? Or if we were to sit down
To a cold dish of stringy greens and the gritty
Loaf of the populace, we'd finger our throat, wouldn't we,
And discover a hidden sore festering in
Our tender mouth, which the vulgarian beet ("It's so
Rough") would be bad for. When pallid fright makes your hair
bristle
You quake all over. Then, if one just brings a torch
Too near you, your blood boils, your eyes glint with temper.
And you give way to such mouthings and behavior
That insane Orestes himself would swear, "This man is mad!"

Satire Four

"Turned to public service?" You can just hear him ask it, that
Philosopher whom a fatal broth of hemlock
Disposed of. Well, Alcibiades, what can you
Lay claim to? Intelligence, of course. Still beardless, you knew
The ropes already. A fine sense of what to tell
And what not to. So when the mob's bile has been worked up
The spirit moves you to still their fever with a noble
Sweep of the hand. Then what do you say? "Citizens,
Romans, there's no justice in that measure, in that other
No virtue, but this one is excellent." For indeed
You've a talent for dangling justice in the twin pans
Of the dubious balance. You can fish out a straight line
From among curves, in spite of a crooked foot-rule,
And you're always ready to pronounce the death sentence on
vice.
You, prospect of well-groomed quite useless skin, how long till
you
Quit twitching your rump at the crooning populace? Better
For you to gulp neat hellebore by the city-full.
What's the highest good, to your way of thinking? Rich dishes

Everlastingly, and nothing to trouble your sunbaths?
You'll find this hag has the same ideas. Then blow your horn:
"I'm Dinomache's son," (that's the way) "I'm a dazzler"—
You, as high-minded as the rag-propping crone
Screeching, "Buy my cabbages," to slatternly house-slaves.
And none tries the descent into himself, no, not one:
Each eyeing the wallet on the shoulders in front of him.
Ask one: "You know Ventidius' place?" "Whose? At Cures?
Old Made-of-Money, who has so much land that a kite
Couldn't fly from one end of it to the other?"
Him? That one? The gods loathe him; his own soul can't stand
him.
Feast days, when the empty yoke's hung up at the crossroads,
It hurts him to scrape the old mould from his tankard;
While the slave-boys celebrate over the victuals, he
Groans, "I hope it will be all right," salting and nibbling
One onion, still in its skin, and sipping with it
His senile vinegar, half dregs, half mother. But suppose
You're lolling oiled and naked in the sun; still some
Total stranger, knocking your elbow, will spit
Savagely at you, "Some habits: plucking your crotch
To make public its secrets—penis and shrivelled testes!
You pamper a perfumed beard on your jaws, why then
Must your cock emerge from an unwhiskered groin? When even
If five wrestlers hauled on the hairs there, attacking
Your flabby buttocks with tweezers shaped for the job,
Still that fern-patch would not be plowed as it should be."
"By turns strike and offer your legs to the arrow"—
That's the rule, we find, which governs our life. There under
Your privates you've a secret sore, but a broad gold belt

Keeps it covered. Well, that's your business: play fast and loose
With your body if you can.
"But the neighbors agree I'm
A good sport. Am I not to believe them?"
If the blood
Leaves your face and your few scruples forsake you
At the mere sight of money, if you'll follow your phallus
Into anything and try any sharp trick to milk
The market, it's pointless to offer the populace
Your ears thirsting for praise. Reject all that is not
Yourself. Let the mob have back what it gave you. Live in
Your own house and learn what a bare lodging it is.

Satire Five

"Oh for a hundred voices"—it's the done thing
For a poet to want them—"one hundred mouths, and the same
Number of tongues"—to recite his own poems, whether
His specialty is the tirade, meant to be mouthed
By some hair-tearing tragedian, or the piece
In which a wounded Parthian extracts a spear-head
From his groin.
"What's all this leading up to? If you're going
To shovel in great poetical gobs like those
It's not surprising if you're in need of a hundred throats
To swallow them. If anyone's anxious to set
Procne's or Thyestes' pot boiling, to provide
That dreary Glyco (playing Tereus) with his supper,
Let loftier bards collect clouds on Mount Helicon.
You're not one to grasp and squeeze the air like a forge-bellows
When they're smelting ore, nor is it your custom to
Caw to yourself, like a crow, a lot of grave drivel,
Nor do you inflate your cheeks till they pop. You employ
The language of common speech, not specially orotund
However trenchant and to the point; you're adept
At ripping into unseemly practices, and can nail

Iniquity precisely with a flick of wit. Take your
Text from these: leave to Mycenaean Thyestes
His banquet of (human) head and members; you stick to
Simple fare."

I'd rather. I don't want to cram my page
Full of ceremonious nothings suitable only
For anchoring smoke. Now as the Muse prompts me,
Addressing myself to you only, Cornutus, I shake
The veils from my breast, dear friend, rejoicing to show you
How great a part of my soul is yours. Strike it, cocking
A sharp ear, and learn how much of it's solid, how much
Is just crusted cosmetics and lip-service. For this one
Theme I would venture to covet those hundred voices:
To make plain to you how fast you are planted in
The whorls of my heart; because I am reminded
Of the limitations of words, when I would disclose all
That is buried, unseen and unsayable, within me.

When, as a shy youth, I put off the purple gown
Of boyhood, and its protection, and hung up my
Amulet to the short-girt gods of the hearth, then when
Companionship held most delight and, robed at last
In a man's white toga, with no part of the city
Closed to me, I could explore as I chose, at that time of life
When the path forks and, with innocent footsteps fetched
To the crossroads, the bashful psyche itself is drawn
Down the branches into division, I consigned
Myself to your charge, Cornutus, and you gathered
My tender years to your Socratic heart. And you applied
The rule with unsuspected cunning, straightening
My crooked ways, and my spirit, laboring to be

Subdued, was molded to the cast of your thought, and took
Form and expression under your shaping thumb.
Oh yes, I remember spending with you the long days
And with you snatching the first hours of the night from
feasting.
We worked as one person, we gave ourselves up to rest
Together and, at ease in each other's presence, relaxed
At the frugal table. I hope you do not doubt
That some powerful affinity knits together
Our two lives, drawn both from the same stars. For whether one
Of the Parcae to whom truth is most precious suspends
Our days in the even Scales, or the same hour which brought
forth
The faithful Twins has disposed between them our friendly
Destinies, or beneficent Jove, in our case
Has overthrown malign Saturn, one constellation
Surely governs us both. Men and the complexions
Of their lives vary in a thousand ways; tastes differ,
And prayers, from one another. Here's a man who trades
Goods from Italy, in the Levant, for wrinkled
Pepper and blanching cumin seed, while that one prefers
To stuff, soak, sleep, get fat, and there's one whose sole interest
Is sport. One gets cleaned out in crap games, another's
Clapped up in cat-houses. But when the stony gout
Has reshaped their knuckles to resemble the burls
Of an old beech, then they groan for their days wasted
Brutishly, they complain that their light was
A will-o-the wisp, and they grieve for a life which
They never knew.
But you have found your joy in growing pale

Over the page night after night, in your ambition
To cultivate the young and in their scrubbed ears sow
The seed of Cleanthes. Oh, you others in your first youth,
And you old men too, from now on seek a firm purpose
For your lives, and make provision for the miseries
Of old age. "I'll do it tomorrow." That's what you'll say
Tomorrow. "You'd grudge me one day?" I tell you, when
Another day is upon us, yesterday's tomorrow
Will have vanished, and look: tomorrow after tomorrow,
Always just out of reach, bearing away your years.
And though its rim comes close to you, and you both revolve
Behind the same wagon-tongue, don't hope to catch up,
Back wheel, strung on the rear axle.
We desire liberty
Though not the sort which any slob can acquire (along with
A chit for one ration of mouldy wheat) by getting
His name listed in the last tribe to be granted
Citizenship. Oh you in whom truth is not even
Conceivable, who think you can twirl a man round once
(Pronouncing the prescribed gibberish) and he'll be
Free. Here, for instance is Dama: two cents' worth of hired
man,
Woozy with flat booze and happy to perjure himself
For a handful of wheat. This one his master accords
The ceremonious whirl and, abracadabra, he
Comes out of the spin a free man, with a first name: he's
Marcus Dama now! And don't tell me you're cagey
About lending him cash—a man with a name like Marcus
For security! You blanch at the thought of having
Marcus try your case? Of course that's a fact: Marcus says so.

Please, Marcus, would you sign these deeds? . . . Well, here's
unmixed
Freedom, at least the sort that passes among us
Under freedmen's liberty caps.
"All right, what else is it
To be free but to be able to live as one pleases?
I can suit myself; am I not more free than Brutus?"
"Your deduction's misleading," a Stoic answers, his
Ears scoured with caustic vinegar. "The rest can pass
If you delete, 'I'm free' and 'I can suit myself.' "
"The praetor touched me with his staff and pronounced me
My own boss, what do you mean I'm not free—as long
As I don't go breaking the statutes in the red-lettered
Code of Masurius?"
If you'll keep your shirt on,
Wipe that sneer off your face and listen, I'll relieve you
Of your old-womanish notions. It's hardly the praetor's place
To provide every fat-head with a fine conscience
And teach him how best to employ his brief span—about
As easy as teaching some ham-fisted boob to melt you
With selections on the harp. It's against reason, as
A little voice in your ear tells you, to let a man
Proceed with something he's bound to make a mess of.
The self-evident law of man and nature limits
The actions of incompetents and half-wits. Try
Making up hellebore prescriptions when you can't
So much as hold the scales steady, and see how long it takes
Till the medical profession cracks down on you. Or let
Some clumping yokel, raw to the regimen of
The morning star, claim command of a vessel; you'll soon hear

His Marine Deity Melicerta declaring
That modesty has deserted the world.
Have the disciplines
Taught you the right way to live and how to discern
The face of truth—not its imitations, which later,
From beneath the gold give out the false clink of copper?
Have you made up your mind what to aim for and what
To steer clear of, marking one with chalk, the other
With charcoal? Are your wishes within reason, is
Your place unpretentious, are you nice to your friends?
Can you close your granaries or open them as you please?
Can you walk past a piece of money stuck in the mud
Without watering at the mouth and swallowing hard
Out of cupidity? When you can honestly claim
All these I'll agree that you're a free man and wise under
Heaven, not merely under the law. However,
If you stick to your old skin (and it's no time, after all,
Since you were baked of the same dough as the rest of us)
With your face all blandness, but the devious fox
Still there in your dull breast, I take it all back,
I reel it in, every last bit. You were born without
A grain of sense. You can't stick out your finger (a little
Thing like that) without doing it wrong. Not all
The frankincense you could set fire to on the altars
Could get one gram of good judgment installed in a fool's head.
Deliberate confusion is impious. If you're
A hick in all other respects, don't fancy you'll be able
To prance and dance like Bathyllus for part of one number.
"I'm free, say what you like." Can you believe it when
You're so easily led by the nose? You don't imagine

That the only master is the one from whom the praetor's wand
Can release you? True, if a voice nags, "Here, boy, take these
Scrapers down to Crispinus at the bath. Get a move on,
Shiftless!" you're nobody's bondsman, you don't have to go,
No influence from without makes you move a muscle.
But if masters spring up within you, there in your
Feeble guts, do you think you'll get off lightly,
Any more than that lash-harried slave with the scrapers?
In the morning you're dead to the world, snoring, when
"Get up," says Avarice, "Come on, up you get."
Nothing doing. But she keeps at it: "I said get up!"
"I can't." "Up." "What for?" "What a question! With those
Dried fish from Pontus to be fetched in, to say nothing
Of the beaver oil, oakum, ebony, frankincense,
Shimmering Coan cloth—and the fresh pepper's come, you
want
To get at that first and grab yours off the camel
Before he's had his drink. Then a bit of haggling (swearing
By the immortals)"—"But Jupiter will hear me." "Listen,
Stupid, get used to life on your uppers, with a thumb-hole
Of your own making worn into your salt-cellar,
Dinner and supper, if you're thinking of keeping in
With Jupiter."
So you get ready: you load up
Your slaves with bales and wine jars, and start bawling, "Get it
On board!" And you're off—almost—in a huge vessel,
Making tracks across the Aegean. There's nothing
To stop you. Only just then sly Luxury nudges you
To one side and puts it to you this way: "Where's the rush?
And where's it taking you (except farther out of

Your senses)? What's the attraction? What can have got you
All overheated like this, and your chest so congested
With virile humors that a whole jug of hemlock
Wouldn't help you? Think of you, *you,* bouncing around
On the billow! You, taking your dinner propped on a thwart
With a coil of rope for a cushion, while from a thick
Wine-pot you catch the reek of a red Veientan vintage
Which has not been improved by its contact with pitch.
What for? To belabor that bit of money
Which you've been nursing along at a quiet five per cent
Till it sweats out an extortionate eleven?
Oh, indulge your genius a bit? Let's taste what pleasures
We can, while life is ours. Soon enough it will be
Ashes, and a shade, and an ended story. Live with
Your death before you, for the hour slips by even now
As I speak."

So what do you do? Hooked two ways and the strain
Tearing you apart, which is it to be? You have no choice but
To submit your two-faced allegiance first to the one
Master, and then, forsaking him, to the other.
And even if, once, you should manage to call
A halt, and refuse to obey the command,
You can't say, "I'm free of my chain." For even a dog
Can contend with his leash till he breaks it, but as he
Runs away you'll observe a good bit of it trailing
From his neck still.

"Davus! Come here! Hurry! This time
I really mean it, I've made up my mind, I'm going
To mend my ways," says Chaerestratus, gnawing his nails raw.
"Do you suppose I want to be a shame and a nuisance

To my starchy relatives? And waste my inheritance
And get a bad name, bawling indecent lyrics,
Blind drunk, with my torch doused, at that whore Chrisidis'
  dripping
Doorway?
            "My boy, I'm happy to hear it. You'd do well
To offer a lamb to the protecting gods. "But do
You think she'll cry, Davus, if I leave her?" "Oh, you were
Only joking! Boy, with that red slipper of hers
She'll make you burn so you won't soon try to weigh out
On your own again, or tear her tight-woven webs!
You storm, you carry on, but if she sends for you, right
In the middle of it, it brings you up short: then it's all
'Now what am I to do? I really can't refuse, can I,
When she sends to ask me, when she positively
Begs me to come?' If you'd really got free of her
Whole and in one piece, you could refuse even so."
Yes, and that's the sort of freedom we're after, not
The kind that can be conferred with a stick and a bit
Of hocus-pocus by any fool lictor.
                                        And that
Smooth candidate gaping for office like a fish
At a fly, would you consider him his own master?
Not missing a trick, littering the place with
Chick-pea tickets for the crowd to scrap over, so that
Basking gaffers may keep harking back to the gorgeous
Floral Games of our day. Isn't that a pretty ambition?
But on Herod's birthday, when the violet-garlanded
Lamps arrayed at their greasy windows have puked out
Fat clouds of smoke, when the tails of swimming tuna

Embrace the red bowls, and the white wine-jugs brim over,
Your lips twitch in silence and you turn pale at the sabbath
Of the circumcised. Other times there are black ghosts,
Dangers attendant on broken eggs, the looming
Emasculate priests of Ceres and the one-eyed priestess
With her rattle, to hammer demons into your frame
If you don't take the prescribed three heads of garlic
Upon rising.
However, bring up such things among
Those varicose centurions and you'll fetch a horse-laugh
Out of some muscle-bound Pulfenius and hear how he'd
Not give a clipped coin for a hundred of your highbrow Greeks.

Satire Six

Has the season, descending into winter,
Fetched you, by now, Bassus, to your Sabine fireside?
Is your strung harp alive to the chastening plectrum,
Oh artisan without peer at ordering in verse
The primal elements of our language and waking
The virile tones of the Latin lyre, oh marvellous
Old man, alive with the merriment of youth and with
Songs, besides, which are gay without being dirty.
For the moment the Ligurian coast and my own
Winter sea offered me their little warmth; from a breach
In the bastion of towering cliffs at the sea's edge
A deep valley here runs inland. As Ennius put it:
"Citizens, you would do well to know the harbor
Of Luna"—speaking in his right mind, when he had
Done dreaming that he was Homer, the Lydian,
Descendant of Pythagoras's peacock.
Here I live, neither troubled by the multitude
Nor flustered by the south wind's ill humors menacing
My flocks, nor miserable because that corner
Of my neighbor's fields is richer than my own. Even
Though men whose birth was beneath mine were to grow rich,

Every one of them, I would still not get all hunched up
And scrawny with fussing over it, nor go without
Sauce for my meat, nor descend to sniffing the seals
Of wine jars to see whether the rank stuff could possibly
Still be swallowed. People aren't all alike. You get twins, with
The same horoscope, turning out to have different
Temperaments. One man makes a habit (but only
On birthdays) of sprinkling his dry greens with brine
Which the sly fellow buys by the cupful—and you can tell
By the way he dribbles the pepper onto the platter
That the stuff is holy. Here's another, a large-mannered
Young man who will shortly have eaten his way through
A huge inheritance. As for me, I try
To make the most of things, without being so lavish
As to feed my freedmen on turbot, nor of so
Sophisticated a palate that I can tell
Hen thrush from cock thrush by the taste.

Live on your own harvest, mill your own grain, that's as it
Should be. Why should you worry? You have only
To harrow again to have another crop on the way.
But obligations nag at your elbow: there's that
Friend who washed up on the Bruttian rocks, in the wreckage
Of his ship, and hauled himself in. He's penniless.
His possessions, accompanied by his useless prayers,
Have settled under the Ionian Sea, and he himself
Is stretched on the beach with the great statues of the gods
From off the vessel's stern strewn round him, while already
The gulls are gathering on the splintered ship's timbers.
Why not divest yourself of a plot of good farmland
And give it to the unfortunate man, and save him

From toting his picture around on a blue board?
Are you hesitant because your heir would be angry
At a cut like that in the property, and after holding
A cheap funeral supper over you, would stuff your bones
Unperfumed into the urn, never bothering
To make sure that the cinnamon was fresh and the cassia
Unmixed with cherry, merely mumbling, "Thought you could
Shave bits off your estate and get away with it,
Did you?" And Bestius will drone on, libelling
The sages of Greece: "That's how it goes, ever since
That neutered brand of philosophy was imported
Into this city with the dates and pepper, our
Farmhands have been getting dainty. Now they've taken
To polluting their gruel with rich oil." But why
Should you worry about this sort of thing once you're on
The other side of the fire? As for you, my heir,
Whoever you are, leave the crowd for a minute and lend me
Your attention.

Haven't you heard, friend? A laurelled
Dispatch has arrived from Caesar, announcing
Victory, the pick of the Germans routed—and already
They're sweeping the dead ashes from the altars, and
Caligula's wife is seeing to the arrangements:
Bouquets of arms for over the gates, costumes for kings,
Yellow wigs for prisoners, and chariots, and monstrous
Models of the Rhine. I'm putting on a little show
Myself, to celebrate the occasion and the gods
And the Emperor's guiding spirit—with a hundred pairs
Of gladiators. Well who says I shouldn't? Who
Would dare to say I shouldn't? God help you if you don't

String along! Oh, and I'm having a largesse of bread,
And meat, and oil distributed to the populace.
Any objections? Speak up. "Oh no," you say, "Not with that
Field full of stones within easy range." Because even
If none of my father's sisters are left, and
I survive all my cousins, and my father's brother
Leaves no great-granddaughters, and my mother's sister
Dies without issue, and my grandmother is survived
By no other descendant, I can always take myself
Over to Bovillae, to the hill of Virbius.
Where there's a wonderful selection of beggars, and there
I'll find me an heir in no time. Manius, for example—
"A son of the soil?" Well ask me who my own grandfather's
Grandfather was. Maybe I can tell you, though again
It might take a moment. But carry it back one more
Generation, then another, and sooner or later
You'll end up with a son of the soil. So if you're going to be
Clannish and stuffy about it, this Manius is really
A sort of great uncle indefinitely removed.
Besides, you've got a nerve, when you're ahead of me, grabbing
For my torch before I've finished my race. Think of me
As your private Mercury, for I come to you like
That god (in the pictures) with a moneybag in my hand.
Don't you want it? Are you determined not to be happy
With what I leave you? "It's not all here." All right, I spent
Some of it for my own uses, but whatever's left
Is all yours. Only you'll get nowhere if you expect me
To give an account of every cent I inherited
Ages ago, from Tadius. And don't come plying me
With fatherly maxims about investing capital

And living on the interest. "But what will be left?"
Left? Here, boy, don't lose a minute: pour out the oil.
Pour, I said! I want my cabbage drowned in it. Maybe
You think I'm going to confine myself on holidays
To smoked cheek of pork and split pig's ear garnished with
  nettles
So that on some future occasion a prodigal unripe
Sot, my heir, his guts stuffed with goose livers, and the fretful
Vein in his privates setting up a restive throbbing,
May piss into a high-born pussy. Or that I should
Abstain till I'm diaphanous so that his paunch
Can jiggle like a priest's.
                                        Go, peddle your soul
For lucre, and haggle, and drag the ends of the earth for
Merchandise. See to it that no one outdoes you
At slapping the fat of Cappadocian slaves, up on the
Auction block. Turn every penny into two. "I have. And
Into three. And four. I've got it up to ten." Well, make
A mark where you want me to stop and I'll inform Chrysippus
That you're the man to finish his unfinishable pile.

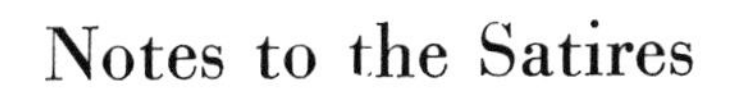

Notes to the Satires

NOTES

(Italicized numbers correspond to the lines of the Latin text; non-italicized numbers, to the lines of the present translation.)

PROLOGUE

1, *1*. The Fountain of Hippocrene, together with Parnassus, Helicon, and the spring at Pirene all belong to the conventional language of the epic poet, all being associated with the Muses and their home in Boeotia. Ever since Hesiod began his *Theogony* by recounting a meeting of his with the Muses, Greek and Latin epic poets have had recourse to the same imaginary description, as a means of defining their inspiration. Here, Persius contemptuously rejects all such nonsense.

SATIRE ONE

9, *4*. *Labeo:* Attius Labeo produced a wretched Latin translation of the Iliad during Persius' lifetime, and the satirist uses him here and farther on at lines 50 and *123* to represent the typically inept poet exalted by popular tastes. For Persius, quality, not popular favor, counts.

22, *15*. Persius describes a typical scene of his time, the public recitation of a poet's works, usually by the poet himself, as here. The satirist treats the situation very harshly and renders it symbolically as homosexual intercourse.

40, *31*. *Romulus' sons:* Romulus was the founder of Rome, and his sons are the noble Romans, sardonically described in this circumlocution. Their physical and mental softness marks a sharp difference between them and their ancestor.

44, *34*. *Phyllis, Hypsipyle:* two typical heroines of tragic romances, whose maudlin stories were so trite—or "rancid" in Persius' words—as to be beneath a real poet's dignity. Such sentimental material formed the basis of much court poetry.

53, *40*. *Hooked nose:* refers not to Persius' physiognomy, but to his manner of sharp criticism. The expression comes from Horace: cf. the phrase in I, *118*.

60, *44*. *Whom I've made up to argue with:* note that Persius openly admits the dramatic fiction behind his dialogue in this poem. Cf. VI, *42*.

63, *47*. *Constructed of horn:* hard like horn, insensitive, unfeeling.

70, *54*. *Client:* Roman custom had produced a social stratification which for many years was very effective. The nobility assumed a position of responsibility towards those of the lower classes; the nobles became patrons, the humbler-born their clients. By imperial times, the system had broken down, and here Persius adopts a typical illustration: the patron, wealthy and thinking himself a true poet, asks his wretchedly poor client for his honest opinion of his poems, at the same time offering the poor man some food and clothes. Obviously, this amounts to sheer bribery, and he automatically hears his poetry exalted.

75, *58*. *Janus:* the god of beginnings and of gates or doorways, who was represented as having two faces looking in both directions.

Stork: refers to a gesture which children made behind people's backs, sticking their forefingers out and going through a pecking motion. It reminded people of the stork's movements, but it signified that someone was crazy.

78, *60*. *Apulian:* Apulia was a province in southern Italy, proverbially hot.

84, *65*. *Nail:* Persius refers to the practice of testing the smoothness of joints by running the fingernail along the surface.

91, 68. *Heroics:* epic poetry, the genre most commonly and lamentably essayed by the poetasters.

95, 72. *Palilia:* the festival on April 21 when Rome celebrated, and still celebrates, her birthday. In Roman times, it involved agricultural ceremonies; hence the allusion to the hay-piles.

96, 73. *Remus:* brother of Romulus, murdered by his brother in a dispute over the founding of the city.

Cincinnatus: One of the great generals of Rome in the mid-fifth century, B.C. Persius mentions one of the famous episodes of his career, when the Romans elected Cincinnatus as dictator to deal with a crisis and had to send the official lictors out into the fields, where their man was humbly plowing, in order to inform him of the honor. Needless to say, Cincinnatus immediately led the Romans to victory.

101, 76. *Bacchanalian Accius, Pacuvius' warty Antiope:* Accius and Pacuvius were two of the greatest tragedians of the second century B.C. Persius cites the famous *Bacchae* of Accius and the *Antiope* of Pacuvius. It is not entirely clear from the Latin who expresses his dislike of the old masters, Persius himself or the poetasters, but it seems more likely that the court poets would be obtuse to the values of archaic Latin poetry than that Persius would; and such men would typically exalt their own works at the expense of their predecessors. Thus, they even sneer at the *Aeneid* in line 96.

112, 85. *Pedius:* it is not known whether this Pedius is a specific criminal or an invented one. A certain Pedius stood trial on a different charge in A.D. 59, and some think that he should be identified with our man here. However, since that would be the only contemporary allusion in the *Satires*, it seems more likely that Persius borrowed the name from Horace, as he did so many other names and phrases.

117, 88. *Ship-wrecked:* Roman sailors, when ruined by shipwreck, often begged through the streets of the city, carrying a picture of the disaster and telling a tearful story to anyone likely to listen and donate to the cause. The practice naturally led to abuses, and Persius compares the artificial sentiments of court poetry with the counterfeit stories of beggars pretending to have suffered shipwreck.

126, 93. *Round out a line:* in the three lines here, Persius illustrates some typical ways in which the court poets abused the conventions of the hexameter and ended the line with a long, meaningless phrase, whose principle value lay in its mellifluous sound, not in its significance.

129, 96. *Arms and the man:* the first words of the *Aeneid*. The court poets of Nero reacted mistakenly against Vergil, unable to attain his greatness.

134ff., 99. The following four lines constitute either a direct quotation or a parody of the typical poetry produced in the Neronian court; in fact, some early writers and their modern followers attribute the lines to Nero himself. For that, the evidence is lacking. On the quality of these lines, in contrast to the style adopted by our satirist, see Introduction, p. 36 f.

Mimallonean and *Bassarid* are learned terms used to refer to the Thracian location of these Dionysiac rites.

154, *113*. *Snakes:* the Romans painted the sign of a snake in places where they did not wish people to relieve themselves.

157, *114*. *Lucilius:* on Lucilius, the inventor of Roman satire, and his most famous victims, Lentulus Lupus and Mucius Scaevola, see Introduction, p. 18 ff.

159, *116*. *Horace:* immediate predecessor of Persius in Roman satire; cf. Introduction, p. 21 ff.

163, *119*. *Mutter a word:* Persius here parodies the story of King Midas and his barber, who, learning that the king had ass's ears and afraid to let the secret out, went out by himself and whispered it to the air. Some scholars have thought that Persius followed the legend more closely and did not generalize about mankind as a pack of asses, but made a vicious insinuation about Nero. He is supposed to have written a different line from that one italicized in the text, and that dangerous passage was subsequently altered, either by Persius himself or by his editors. I do not find the theory convincing; rather, the satirist's expressed contempt for mankind fits perfectly his attitude as evidenced in other Satires.

169-70, *123-4.* *Cratinus, Eupolis:* with Aristophanes, they were the three most famous writers of Old Comedy, and as such Horace cites them. To the Roman mind, they connoted a sharp attack on vice, a fearless but righteous onslaught. When Persius mentions them here as the proper reading matter for his audience, he means that he adopts their manner.

174, *127.* *Greek slippers:* buskins used by the tragic actors.

175, *128.* *One-Eye:* possibly an allusion to Nero, who made a similar remark about one of his courtiers who was one-eyed.

177, *130.* *Hick magistrate:* an aedile at Arrezzo according to the Latin. The aediles were responsible for checking the weights of market-men; and this one seems to be puffed up with his petty authority.

188, *134.* *Calliroe:* The Latin here is very compressed. Literally, it may be rendered: "In the morning I give these people the edict, after lunch Calliroe." Because of Persius' brevity and a plethora of Calliroes, this particular Calliroe has been the subject of controversy. One tenable interpretation: Calliroe is the heroine of a sentimental mime, who stirs the tears of the stupid spectators by her erotic adventures and passionate language. A woman of the same name is the heroine of the earliest extant Greek novel, *Chaereas and Calliroe,* written by Chariton possibly about this same time. In any case, Calliroe here represents a maudlin work of low art, the very opposite of Persius' literary ideal, both in subject and language.

SATIRE TWO

1, *1.* *White stone:* the stone or pebble was used for reckoning, and the color white signified happiness and prosperity. *Macrinus:* some friend of Persius, who is here used to represent the appropriate way to approach the gods; otherwise, his name is unknown to us.

3, *3.* *Genius:* the tutelary spirit of each individual.

7-8, *5.* *Pots which breathe:* note the typical violent metaphor.

21, *14.* *Nerius:* a fictitious name taken from Horace *Serm.* II, 3, 69.

21-22, *15.* It seems to have been a standard ritual for penitents to bathe in the cold Tiber.

27, 19. *Staius:* a proverbially corrupt judge, probably not of Persius' time.

40, 26. *Etruscan witch:* the Etruscans were masters in the interpretation of certain natural omens, especially those supposedly present in lightning and in animal livers. Persius here refers to the typical instance employed by so many philosophers to disprove the active engagement of the deity in human affairs: the lightning does not usually strike the guilty, but hits at random, often the good rather than the evil.

51-52, 36. *Licinus* and *Crassus:* typical men of wealth a hundred years earlier.

54, 38. *Roses:* these symbolize magical powers of success.

56, 40. *White dress:* the proper costume for pious exercise, as today.

62, 44. *Mercury:* the Roman god peculiarly responsible for mercantile activities, sharp practices, and the prosperity that often results therefrom.

74, 54. *Sweat:* another conceit of Persius, by which he refers to two normal symptoms of excitement, namely, sudden sweat and the rapid beating of the heart (in the left breast).

75, 55. *Gilded:* one of the special votive offerings in Rome consisted of donating a sum of gold, with which a statue of cheaper metal—here, the face only—could be gilded.

77, 56. *Bronze brotherhood:* a disputed passage, but Persius seems to wish to convey his prejudice against mercenary prayers by quoting them in exaggerated form. The man does not really believe in the gods, but sneeringly describes them as a group of bronze statues, not active personalities. And yet he wants to make sure of his success and so will reward whichever god seems to aid him!

79, 59. *Numa:* the second king of Rome, following Romulus the founder; he was proverbially simple and pious, not in the least concerned with advancing his wealth or power. Saturn's associations are also simplicity; under him occurred in myth that Golden Age when men were content with little, when gold was unknown, when wars were unheard of.

81, 60. The ceremonies of the Vestal virgins continued to use the traditional material from early times, hence the old Etruscan pottery rather than glittering gold.

87, 64. *Cassia:* a spice used to conceal the poor quality of olive oil which unscrupulous traders were currently marketing. Similarly, other merchants were adulterating the precious purple dye, imported from Tyre, with cheaper and less fast coloring. Calabria, on the heel of Italy, produced the finest wool-bearing sheep.

95, 70. Girls about to be married presented to Venus their dolls as a symbol of the end of childish innocence and the assumption of maturity. As Persius notes, Venus would hardly make much use of such gifts.

97, 72. *Messala:* one of the great nobles under the Augustan regime, consul in 31 B.C. and patron of poets like Tibullus and Ovid. He had a son who seems to have degenerated considerably from his father's magnificence. However, it is unlikely that Persius here refers to a living Messala; rather, as in other cases, the satirist uses a typical name to represent graphically a typical moral condition.

SATIRE THREE

3, 3. *Falernian:* one of the finest Italian wines, grown in northern Campania.

4-5, 5. *Fifth mark:* the sundial marks what would be equivalent to our 11:00 A.M.

11, 9. *Arcadia:* in the central Peloponnese of Greece, where the finest asses were produced. Of course, the braying of asses connotes unpleasant noise.

12, 10. *Hairless parchment:* parchment, being made of animal skins, had to have the hairs taken off before use.

37-38, 28. *Tuscan ancestor:* Romans liked to boast of their ancient origins, and the Etruscans corresponded to the Pilgrim fathers in America. Persius, who may well have had some Etruscan ancestors of his own, here expresses his contempt for empty boasting over genealogy. A man should stand on his own feet.

38, 29. *Parade:* a regular assemblage of the men of equestrian rank.

42, 31. *Natta:* another typical name drawn from Horace; Natta was the epitome of extravagance.

52, 39. *Bull of Sicily:* Phalaris, tyrant of Agrigento in the early Sixth Century B.C., constructed a hollow bronze bull, into which he put his enemies. Then, he built a fire around the statue and listened to the moans of his dying prisoners, sounds which emerging from the mouth of the bull resembled the bellowing of the animal.

53, 40. *Sword:* of Damocles, another allusion to the tyrant's existence as drawn from a typical instance.

61, 44. *Eyes bleary:* schoolboys had their ways of malingering in Persius' day as well as now. Olive oil in the eyes gave them an inflamed appearance which suggested serious illness; in any case, it seemed to render inadvisable the chore of memorizing.

62, 45. *Cato's death-speech:* even more than our students today, the Romans acquired ability with their language by memorizing and repeating famous speeches, or by inventing speeches whch might have been delivered on certain important occasions. The occasion when Cato killed himself at Utica, rather than submit to the ambitions of Julius Caesar, was one of these.

67, 46. Dice was a favorite game of Roman boys. Double six won, while a pair of ones always lost. Note the other games described.

72, 54. *Porch:* the Painted Porch or Stoa in Athens, where the Stoic philosophy originally began, that is, where Zeno first collected students. Despite the language, Persius here exalts Stoicism as the ideal for all young men.

77, 56. *Pythagoras' Letter of Life:* Pythagoras in the fifth century B.C. developed a parable from the shape of the capital upsilon, which resembled our Y. Life, he said, confronts us with many choices, and we come to forks in the road (shaped like the Y) where we have to decide whether to take the hard, but honest, way or what seems like the path of least resistance.

87, 63. *Hellebore:* the standard purgative of ancient times. Persius uses physical sickness in this Satire and elsewhere to symbolize spiritual disease, a favorite metaphor of moralists.

99, *74*. *Umbrians:* like the Marsians, clients of some shrewd lawyer, who successfully defends their case. Coming from the rural portions of Italy as they do, they reward him lavishly with the produce of their lands. Another typical instance.

104, *77*. *Goat-odored centurion:* the goat traditionally stinks, and the Centurion typified stupidity for the Romans. The combination here is a most prejudicial description of ignorant antagonism towards philosophc truth.

106, *79*. *Arcesilaus:* Founder of the Middle Academy in the third century B.C. He, Solon, and probably Epicurus ("prostrate old wheeze") serve to represent Philosophy as the stupid centurion comprehends it.

123, *93*. *Surrentine:* another fine wine, grown around the modern region of Sorrento.

136-37, *103*. *Trumpet and torches:* Persius here describes a typical Roman funeral. In other words, he quickly jumps to the point where the sick man has died.

140, *106*. *Freedmen:* it was often the practice for a Roman nobleman to leave a provision in his will whereby certain slaves were freed. It is now the day after the invalid's death, so his slaves are "yesterday's freedmen"; they wear a certain pointed cap as a sign of their status.

156, *118*. *Orestes:* the mythological character who, because he killed his own mother in a state of mental uncertainty and then suffered attacks of insanity thereafter, typically represented madness. Persius' conclusion suggests that he has compressed the Stoic paradox into this line, that his theme throughout the Satire has been not merely that we are all "sick" (except for the Stoic), but more specifically that we are all "mad."

SATIRE FOUR

1-2, *1*. *That philosopher:* Socrates. Persius elaborates on Plato's dialogue, *Alcibiades I* for the first third of the Satire. In that dialogue, Socrates discussed with his pupil Alcibiades the qualities which should make up a true statesman.

17, 16. *City-full:* in the Latin, Persius cites the most famous source of hellebore in antiquity, the port-towns in Phocis and Thessaly, both called Anticyra.

21, 20. *Dinomache:* Alcibiades' mother, relative of Pericles. Alcibiades relied greatly on his mother's family for his political start.

25, 24. *Wallet on the shoulders:* another proverbial situation. Men are imagined to carry two wallets, one with their virtues on their chests, another with their vices on their backs. Under these circumstances, it is most usual for a stranger, walking behind, to see the wallet containing the vices and to generalize about a man from them alone.

26-7, 25-6. *Vettidius:* unknown and most probably a type for miserliness.

Cures was a village just outside Rome, the home once of Numa Pompilius.

27, 26. *Kite:* another proverbial expression. If the swift-flying bird, the kite, could not cover the area of property in a day, then the miser must have possessed an incalcuable amount.

30, 28. *Yoke:* the farmer hung his yoke at the crossroads on festivals, especially the Compitalia, in honor of the protecting deities, the Lares, and as a symbol of his rest from labor.

59, 52. *House:* a typical metaphor for moralists. Live in your own house, that is, know thyself and depend upon the solid values which you certainly know to exist within your own character. Cf. the statement of the theme in line 23.

SATIRE FIVE

6, 4. *Parthian:* the Parthian warrior, who plagued the Roman frontier in the East from the middle of the first century B.C. on, constituted a typical topic for the epic poet, as Persius here contemptuously indicates.

12-14, 7-9. *Procne, Thyestes, Glyco:* Procne was the heroine of a grisly myth which was developed by the tragedians and also by Ovid. Angry at her husband's raping of Philomela, her sister, she killed and dismembered her only son and lured her husband Tereus into eating the cooked flesh. A similar story is told of Thyestes, except that he played the role of the father eating his children. Seneca wrote a tragedy entitled *Thyestes,* so Persius has a contemporary interest, if not a specific play, in mind. Glyco was a well-known actor of the first century A.D., a proverbial specialist in the more melodramatic roles.

Mount Helicon: as in the Prologue, stands for the meretricious associations of Grand Poetry. Persius wants none of this; he wants the hard truth of Stoicism.

29, *23.* *Cornutus:* Persius' beloved tutor; cf. Introduction, p. 9 ff. Here follows the celebrated tribute of pupil to master, which renders Cornutus almost into a Roman Socrates, as suggested by the expression in line *37,* "Socratic heart."

41, *31.* *Amulet:* a Roman boy wore an amulet about his neck to guard him against evil spirits. It constituted a symbol of his youth, so that, when he took it off and dedicated it to the Lares, he had reached adolescence, approximately the age of sixteen.

61, *48.* *Parcae:* the Fates. Persius here employs various astrological themes to indicate the identity between his fate and Cornutus': the even Scales, the Twins—both signs in the Zodiac—and the similar influence of the planets Jove and Saturn upon them.

82, *63.* *Cleanthes:* celebrated Stoic of the third century B.C., pupil of Zeno. Cornutus teaches the ideal Stoic doctrine, and Persius totally embraces that creed.

95, *74.* *Chit:* the Romans developed a system of dole whereby citizens received a *tessera,* a chit, which entitled them to corn, wine, oil, even admission into the theatre. Thus, any slave, once freed, became entitled to such a privilege.

103, *75.* *Ceremonious whirl:* in the ritual of emancipation, the slave was turned around, tapped with a special staff, and then acquired the title of freedman.

111, *82.* *Liberty caps:* cf. III, *106.*

114, *85.* *Brutus:* father of Roman liberty, the hero who drove the Tarquins out of the city and established the Republic, serving as one of the first consuls.

116, *86*. *Ears scoured:* a typical and laudatory description of the Stoic ideal, odd as it may seem. Cf. Introduction, p. 39 f.

118, *88*. *Praetor:* Roman official particularly responsible for legal and judicial matters.

121, *90*. *Masurius:* Sabinus, great jurist of Tiberius' time who produced a voluminous Code of Justice, therefore constituted a typical reference for legal rights.

138, *103*. *Melicerta:* god of the sea, who protests at the ignorance of this pilot.

165, *123*. *Bathyllus:* a famous dancer; like Glyco, a typical reference.

203, *147*. *Veientan:* very poor wine, grown at Veii some fifteen miles outside Rome.

223, *161*. *Davus:* Persius here follows Horace in developing a scene from Terence's famous comedy *Eunuchus*. The scene depicts the indecisive condition of Chaerestratus, torn between his passion for Chrysis and his perfect awareness of her faithlessness; he is the typical slave to passion.

250, *177*. *Tickets:* special *chits* (cf. V, *74*) scattered to the crowd during celebrations donated by some public official; such donations became the curse of Rome under the Empire, as the populace grew to depend upon them and demanded them on the slightest pretext.

252, *178*. *Floral Games:* the Floralia, a licentious festival in early Spring.

253, *180*. *Herod:* Herod Agrippa, dead now some twenty years, used as a typical Jewish ruler. All the Jews, says Persius, religiously celebrate Herod's birthday, and the interlocutor feels the tug of superstition also.

260, *186*. *Ceres:* in the form of Cybele, an Eastern goddess, she exacted fanatic worship from her followers; significantly, her priests were eunuchs. The one-eyed goddess is Isis, originating in Egypt, patroness of another very popular and emotional cult. Cybele had entered Rome early in the second century B.C. Isis arrived later, but by Persius' day there were at least two impressive cult-centers for her worship in Rome, of which we have ample remains today, most notably in the form of some of the obelisks that grace the piazzas of modern Rome. Persius' allusions to superstition convey more actuality than most of his other details.

265, *189*. *Centurions:* the same illustration of block-headed stupidity as in III, *77* ff.

SATIRE SIX

2, *1*. *Bassus:* Caesius Bassus, successful lyric poet of the day, close friend of Cornutus and Persius, editor and publisher of the Satires after Persius' early death.
Sabine fireside: like Horace, his predecessor in lyric, Bassus retired from Rome in the winter to write poetry, apparently to a villa near modern Subiaco.

9, *6*. *Ligurian coast:* Persius has withdrawn to Luna, as he states below in line 9. Luna was located at the northernmost point of Etruria, close to modern La Spezia.

12, *10*. *Ennius:* greatest Roman poet prior to Vergil, founder of many Roman genres, including epic and satire. Persius plays with a quotation from one of his works, probably an early portion of his famous epic, the *Annales*. If so, the Luna there referred to would have nothing to do with the Etrurian port, but would be the moon itself. Ennius had a weird dream by which he represented himself as the spiritual heir of Homer, having experienced metempsychosis or metamorphosis, as Homer's spirit passed through that of Pythagoras' peacock—Pythagoras particularly developed this theory of spiritual survival—ultimately into Ennius' soul. The whole conception aroused the amusement of later writers, as here, and yet Ennius did fulfill in Roman literature a near-Homeric role.

43, *27*. *Bruttian:* Bruttium was the province including the toe of Italy. Someone washed up on its rocks might well have been caught in the severe storms of the Straits of Messina.

46, *29*. *Ionian Sea:* that section of the Mediterranean which ran along the bottom of the foot of Italy across to the coast of Greece.

52, *32*. *Toting his picture:* the same type of begging as in I, 88 ff.

55, *33*. *Funeral:* other features of the funeral to complement the scene in III, *103* ff. It was customary for the heir to provide for the funeral, to donate perfumes for the pyre and to invite the dead man's friends and relatives to a banquet in memory of the deceased. A stingy or angry heir might well abbreviate these rites.

60, *37*. *Bestius:* the name comes from Horace. He represents the type who blames all the country's ills on foreigners, regardless of the true causes and of the good things—like the Stoic philosophy—which the Greeks have introduced.

71, *43*. *Caesar:* this vignette comes closest to a satirical attack of the Juvenalian type; it is the sole clear political allusion in the six Satires, and typically it involves the Emperor Caligula, dead since 41, some twenty years. Caligula decided to emulate his predecessors, all of whom had attained prominence in victories over the threatening German tribes, and proclaimed a campaign in 39. Nothing came of it but a series of fantastic and demented actions culminating in the counterfeit triumph here described. Not having defeated any Germans, Caligula had to disguise some men as German prisoners, contrive booty, and devise some fake pictures of the feats which had never taken place. However, the occasion proved an excellent pretext for levying tribute on the rich; even though the rich man here talking with his heir realized perfectly well the situation, he had to act his part in order to preserve his life, and it was his duty to assist the triumph financially. In fact, as he threatens, he could have done even more besides his "little show" of gladiators; he might have distributed vast amounts of food to the poor as part of the general festivities.

91, *55*. *Bovillae:* a town on the slopes of the Alban Hills, in that section described here by Persius as the "Virbian hill" because of its association with the god Virbius. As one travelled south on the Appian Way, one had to pass over a section of the Alban Hills, and the highway climbed steeply for a long time in order to reach quickly the crest of the hills. Naturally, all traffic of carriages and wagons was slowed down, and accordingly beggars found this long hill one of the best places to carry out their profession, since they had, so to speak, a captive audience for a while. Persius says that, if the true heir spurns his paltry inheritance, he can always find a beggar who will take him up on it; and ultimately we are all related.

103, *62*. *Mercury:* god of business and quick profits, cf. II, *44*.

126, *77*. *Cappadocian:* some of the finest and strongest slaves, not necessarily the brightest, came from Cappadocia in eastern Asia Minor.

129, *80*. *Chrysippus:* the most important Stoic after the founder Zeno, a voluminous writer, a man who posed—as indicated here—impossible problems, using the chain of logical arguments called the sorites, a Greek derivative from the word meaning "pile" or "heap." A typical sorites, attributed to Chrysippus by Diogenes Laertius, runs as follows: "If you never lost something, you have it still; but you never lost horns, *ergo* you have horns." Just as it was impossible to solve Chrysippus' sorites—leaving aside the illegitimate major premise—so the avaricious can never satisfy his desire for wealth, no matter how much his possessions are multiplied.